DEDICATION

I dedicate this book to my family for their unwavering love and support; to my martial arts instructors masters Martin Ducker and Alison, and to Christine Gray who was like a mum to me.

THE UNWANTED

JOURNEY FROM ABUSED CHILD TO MARTIAL ART MASTER

GIFT

DON MACKENZIE

CONTENTS

AUTHOR'S NOTE

Everything you're about to read is exactly how I remember my life - the words that never came out of my mouth, but instead remained trapped in my mind, slowly breaking me from the inside.

It's my story, a life that has been a constant war. It's about creating success from a tough start. It's about my battle with CPTSD, mental health, and the journey from darkness into light. Above all else, it's about how we can overcome the things we're afraid to talk about, and how realising the way to heal from the past is to talk openly about everything that broke us.

All the amazing things I've achieved in my life have been shaped by the trauma of my past, as well as the love, support, and kindness of the people who made all the difference.

True strength comes from deep within, supported by the people who love and care for us.

CHAPTER 1:

THE NEUROLOGIST'S OFFICE

I was sitting outside the neurologist's office, a million thoughts per second flying through my head in an endless cycle of repetitive "what if" scenarios. None of them were good. All of them involved me dying or being seriously ill from some strange brain disorder. It's funny what runs through your head when you're thinking about your own mortality. My thoughts raced: How will my family survive without me? What is wrong with me? It must be serious, after twelve or so years of progressively worsening symptoms.

My brain was whirling, yet I noticed every tiny detail of the waiting room, every small sound. I had already resigned myself to whatever would be. I had accepted the universe's plan for me, whether good or bad. After all, the journey had already been a lifelong struggle. Everything I'd been through up to that point had been so tough and mentally draining. It had drained me to the core.

Like I said, I was strangely at ease with whatever might come. My brain, I would later learn, was hard-wired for catastrophising.

1

"Mr Mackenzie," a voice rang out, snapping me back to reality and out of my obsessive looping thoughts.

"Mr Mackenzie," I heard again.

"Yes, that's me," I replied.

"In you come and have a seat," the neurologist said.

I walked in and took a seat in his office. He introduced himself, then asked if it was okay for a medical student to sit in with us. She was currently training in the UK, and it would be good experience for her to hear my case.

"No worries at all," I said.

Once again, my catastrophic thinking was spinning. I couldn't even tell if I was really in his office or just dreaming. Everything felt surreal. It was like a strange, detached experience where I could just about tell it was real, but my brain kept screaming that none of it was. The only thing anchoring me to reality was my senses and some strange inner knowing that this was actually happening. It was a weird feeling. My brain was processing hundreds of scenarios every second, and I felt totally dissociated.

"Mr Mackenzie, I have read your medical notes. Can you tell me, in your own words, what's been going on?"

"Yeah, no worries at all," I said, glancing between him and the student who was already observing me closely. I could see she was studying me, and I wondered what she might be thinking. I also noticed the neurologist had a pocket penlight in his upper coat pocket, and for some reason it fascinated me. By this point, I had scanned every inch of his office, down to a small crack in the wall to the left of me. My brain latched onto that crack, thinking about how I could easily fix it with some filler. Then I wondered

2

why nobody had sorted it. My brain was off again, tumbling with thoughts. I had no idea what "repetitive thoughts" were at that point. I just thought that's how I was.

"Well," I began, "it started about twelve years ago, just before Christmas..."

I gave the neurologist a brief summary. I told him how I'd been sitting in the living room, the Christmas tree lights flickering, when I suddenly felt unwell. My vision went blurry, strange light patterns flickered in my eyes, and I had a pounding headache. Pauline thought it might be a migraine.

But I kept it brief. I didn't tell him everything. Not yet.

The truth was it was terrifying. That night, I hadn't said a word. I went to lie down alone. My phone screen turned into meaningless shapes, like a puzzle I couldn't solve. Lightning flashes ripped through my vision. I was convinced I was having a stroke. That was my brain. Always leaping to disaster.

The following morning, I felt worse. Drained. Foggy. Like my brain had been fried. Then came the pins and needles: left arm, face, eyes. A week later, I saw my GP. She also thought it was a migraine. "Give it time," she said. But time didn't help.

Weeks passed, but the pressure in my head never eased. Random burning spots appeared on my skin, like molten metal had been poured into me. Nothing made sense. I went back to the doctor. More tests. More pills. Still, nothing changed.

"After that," I told the neurologist, "I saw a few GPs. They all said different things - migraine, maybe stress tension headaches. I was given medication, but nothing helped. That's when I realised, I needed to push for answers."

What I didn't say was that I'd tried everything. One doctor prescribed me Pizotifen, even though I hate taking medication. I slept for twenty hours and woke up feeling like I was falling backwards off a building. My body zapped like it had a loose wire.

The cognitive fog was the worst. Teaching martial arts became a struggle. I couldn't remember students' names. The more I panicked, the worse it got. Even light made it worse. Fluorescents left me dizzy and slurring my words, like I was drunk.

By then, I'd seen five doctors. One even said my symptoms didn't exist. That stung more than I let on. I hate when people don't believe what I'm telling them.

"One doctor thought it could be mini strokes," I told the neurologist. "Or possibly MS. But another kept mentioning stress. He asked me about my background and childhood."

That was the first time a doctor had ever asked.

I shocked myself by opening up. I let it all pour out. He had read my medical notes and could see the symptoms I'd described over the years to different GPs. For the first time, someone took them all seriously, as a whole.

I told him about my childhood. About the abuse. The children's home. I hadn't meant to. But I was worn down. Absolutely broken inside. Tears rolled down my cheeks. Something opened up, and the flood of memories came flying out - stuff I had never told anyone. A mixture of shame, guilt, and relief. An unburdening. I knew it was killing me from the inside out.

He mentioned something I'd never heard before:

CPTSD. Complex Post-Traumatic Stress Disorder.

He said it might explain the dreamlike states I'd experienced since childhood. The brain fog. The hypervigilance. The ruminating thoughts. The sudden tears. The panic attacks. All of it.

I nodded. My eyes were red from crying. I stayed silent, trying to process what he was saying. But I didn't really understand.

Back then, I didn't think PTSD was something people like me got. I thought it only happened to soldiers who had been to war. But PTSD can come from short-term trauma. CPTSD is from prolonged exposure to threat - years of it. It's classified as worse, and harder to treat.

"Anyway," I said to the neurologist, "that's when I finally asked for a referral. That's how I ended up here."

"You know what," I added, "this will sound weird, but I can't even tell that I'm here talking to you. It feels unreal, like I'm dreaming. I know it's happening, but it doesn't feel real."

He said, "That doesn't sound weird. It's called dissociation. I had it when I was at university."

It was the first time a professional didn't look at me like I was making things up.

"Mr Mackenzie, I think you have Functional Neurological Disorder," he said. "Also known as FND. As well as CPTSD."

My heart raced. My mind went into overdrive. What did he just say? What is FND? Is it serious? Can you live with it? Am I going to die? How bad can it be?

"What is FND?" I asked.

He replied, "Think of your brain as the computer and your nervous system as the software. They're not communicating properly. You also have pronounced dissociation. Most people get it occasionally. You experience it almost all the time. That's unusual."

At the time, I couldn't fully take in what he was saying. For more than a decade, I'd been told it was complex migraine syndrome, stress headaches, possibly MS, or small brain strokes. All of that had been ruled out.

The symptoms affected my short-term memory. Things I'd just said a minute ago would vanish. The harder I tried to remember, the further the thoughts would slip away.

Since then, I've read extensively on Functional Neurological Disorder and its symptoms. I understand now why I developed it and how it links to my life. I consider myself lucky. FND can be extremely debilitating. Even though there's nothing physically wrong, the miscommunication between brain and nervous system can cause severe issues. Some people end up in wheelchairs, unable to walk. Symptoms include limb weakness, seizures, tremors, tics, chronic pain, and sensory symptoms. Dissociation is also a part of FND.

The exact cause is unknown. Sigmund Freud called it a conversion disorder. It's thought to be triggered by extreme stress or trauma. After living with it for over twelve years, I have no doubt mine came from childhood trauma and abuse.

Dunbar hospital where I was born 1970

Me at the childrens home

Thurso childrens home as it is now

CHAPTER 2:
MRS NOBODY

I was born on the eighteenth of May 1970 in Dunbar Hospital, in the most northerly town on the UK mainland - a place called Thurso. It's the last stop on the railway line from the south and is over 500 miles from London. Once an important Norse port, Thurso is an ancient town with a history stretching back before the era of Norse or Orcadian rule in Caithness. It was a hub for fishing and farming, and later, trade.

Interestingly, the senior detective in the Jack the Ripper case, Donald Swanson (1848–1934), came from Thurso.

When I was growing up, Thurso had a population of about ten and a half thousand. This was largely due to the Dounreay nuclear power plant, which served as the UK centre of fast reactor research and development from 1955 until 1994 and is now being decommissioned. There was also a United States Navy radio station at Forss, near Thurso, built in 1962 to improve communication with the USA and NATO forces in the North Atlantic. This brought many American servicemen and women - and their families - to Thurso and the surrounding area.

My mum died of cancer when I was just two years old. My dad, who was married to someone else and had his own family, didn't want anything to do with me. Before she passed, my mum was too unwell to care for me or my siblings. Most of us were placed in a children's home in Lybster, Caithness.

There was me, my older brother Andrew, and my older sisters Kathleen and Christine. My eldest sister Ann and eldest brother Geordie didn't go to the home, as they were older. I don't remember anything about Lybster, and I'm glad. Everyone I've spoken to about it says nothing but terrible things. Some won't even talk about it because the memories are too painful.

My first real memory is of walking home from Thurso nursery, holding someone's hand. I don't remember who it was or why it stands out, but it's the earliest memory I have. By then, we'd been moved to the Thurso children's home on Ormile Road. Lybster had either shut down or was about to.

The next memory is of my first day at school - Miller Academy - and meeting Tommy Reid, who would become a lifelong friend. That first day didn't go to plan. During the first morning break, when all the kids went outside to play, I persuaded Tommy that we should hide at the bottom of the hill and not go back in when the bell rang.

When it did ring and the other kids returned to class, we stayed hidden, heads down but still able to see the classroom. The teacher came out, worried, calling our names. We stayed silent. Then the headmaster and a couple of other teachers joined in, searching and shouting for us. Still, we didn't move.

Eventually, one of them found us. They were furious. We got shouted at and punished for what they called beyond stupid behaviour. But to me, it wasn't anything new. I'd heard it all before.

Now, looking back, I understand why I did it. At the time, I thought it was just a funny story - kids being kids. But years later, through trauma counselling, I came to understand that everything I did was shaped by my childhood experiences. Hiding was a coping mechanism. It was how I dealt with authority and unfamiliar situations.

I realised early on that school was going to be difficult. I hated being shouted at, and I had a deep mistrust of any authority figure. But I knew I had no choice. I had to be there.

I used to arrive at school very early, always the first one there. I'd wait for the janitor, then help him with the milk run. Back then, every child got a mini bottle of milk daily. I'd help organise the crates and distribute the bottles. Anything to get away from the children's home for a while - and more importantly, from one particular staff member. I won't call her a carer, because she was the opposite. She was a monster.

I thought long and hard about what name to give her in this book. I was advised not to use her real name, which annoyed me. The truth is the truth, and any child who lived in that home at the time knows exactly who she was. Most still struggle to even say her name. Some have bad dreams and intrusive thoughts because of her. So, I will call her Mrs Nobody. Because to me, she is a nobody.

She was already an older woman when she began working at the children's home on Ormile Road - which we kids just called "the home." But it was anything but. A home should be safe and nurturing, especially for kids who had already gone through traumatic events.

Under Mrs Nobody, the home was a place of fear. The smallest mistake, real or imagined, brought swift and brutal punishment. She was a battle-axe. Chain-smoked. Drank whisky. And seemed to have a deep hatred for kids. Especially kids like us - the "useless, broken, unloved ones," as she liked to remind us. She had her own children, whom she thought the sun shone out of.

At the time, there were usually seven to twelve kids in the home. My brother Andrew, my sisters Kathleen and Christine, and I were all there after Lybster closed. I was around two or three when we arrived, and although I don't remember Lybster, I later spoke to people who were there, and their stories were horrific. I'm grateful I was too young to remember.

But I do remember Thurso, and the fear. I had a terror of the dark, and Mrs Nobody used it against me. Not all abuse is physical. She used every form. And for me, the worst wasn't the beatings, though they were bad - daily slaps, punches, being hit with whatever was nearby. Over time, you become hardened to it. It becomes normal.

What was worse was the constant anxiety. Never knowing when the next punishment was coming. Always being on high alert. Monitoring everything I said or did.

That wears you down. And almost every kid who grew up under Mrs Nobody paid the price later in life.

Over the years, I found and spoke with many of the kids who were there. We talked about her and the lasting impact she had on our lives. Many have struggled with alcohol or drug abuse, nightmares, relationship difficulties, self-harm, criminal convictions. I learned that these are all common in people with CPTSD.

My brother Andrew never showed emotion. He became immune to the beatings. That infuriated Mrs Nobody. She couldn't break him. But she tried.

It's difficult to describe what life was like then, as so much was happening that it all kind of blends into one big event. As I said, for us, that was normal life, as strange as that may sound. We knew no different, and no one was coming to save us.

Mrs Nobody had complete and utter control over every facet of our lives, like what time we got up, what we got for breakfast - if we even got breakfast - as one of her little punishments was depriving us of food for a period of time. I lost count of the number of times either I, or one of the other kids, would be sent to bed after school with no dinner or breakfast until the following day. That stayed with me throughout my life, as even now I finish my dinner in three minutes flat - way before anyone else. If I go out with my family for a meal, I'm always the first to finish my food and start to feel a bit on edge if we have to sit longer than a short amount of time. Eating so quickly all the time has led to IBS and digestive problems too. That's the legacy of abuse - it never truly leaves us. Anxiety and a sense of dread were beaten into me from a young age, and they're with me every second of every day. That constant sense that something really wrong is going to occur at any minute is a draining way to live your life, but that's just how it is.

At the dinner table in the home, Mrs Nobody would sit at the top of the table, and her husband, who I will call *Flat Cap Man*, sat at the other end. He was a very quiet man who never really spoke - I think he was a bit afraid of his wife, to be honest. Mealtimes were a terrifying event for the kids in the home because you had to sit in the presence of Mrs Nobody with nowhere to hide, and you had to watch everything you did and spoke.

A kid wetting herself at the dinner table out of sheer fear, and Mrs Nobody, with great delight, used it to humiliate and ridicule her in front of all the other kids. She was made to clean it up on her hands and knees.

That wasn't shocking to us kids, as a few of them wet the bed, or one girl even defecated in the corner of the living room. Like I said, it's amazing what becomes your normal when you see it all the time.

Now, the dinner table had its rules as set by Mrs Nobody. For example – if they served you stew, even if you hated it you had to stay at the dinner table until you finished whatever was put in front of you - absolutely no exceptions. If you didn't finish it, there was a price to be paid.

One night, we were having a meal, and Andrew hated what it was - I think it was sausage rolls, if I remember correctly. Anyway, we called it "Operation Day," as my brother would pick and prod and dissect the sausage roll.

14

We all knew he would never eat it, as you couldn't make my brother do anything he didn't want to do.

This time, there was the usual battle of wills between my brother and Mrs Nobody, and she had had enough, as Andrew was the most stubborn person in the world.

Mrs Nobody flew into a rage and said, "You will sit there until you finish your meal." She made my brother sit for three days, morning till night, with that sausage roll in front of him, and my brother never gave in,

Eventually she did.

Strange what small victories mean in a place like that.

My older brother was like that - nothing would beat him, nothing. There were times when Mrs Nobody would fly into a rage and try to force-feed you whatever was on your plate, but one thing was for sure: if you didn't eat, you were going to be punished.

At the time, the kids devised ways to get through mealtimes, whether it was another kid eating what you didn't like off your plate after Mrs Nobody had left the table, or you would pocket anything you could and dispose of it down the toilet.

Our favourite method was feeding the food to Rusty, the dog in the children's home. All the kids adored him - he was a golden retriever. He would come up under the table after Mrs Nobody had left, and we would feed him our food.

Rusty ballooned in weight, as he was getting loads of food from us kids, and the staff in the home put him on a diet, unable to understand why he was getting so big.

Mrs Nobody used to slam her fist on the table and shout in Gaelic to *shut up*, or she would roar in English, "Kids should be seen, not heard."

I used to try and be invisible when Mrs Nobody was on one of her rants. She could fly into a rage over nothing. I actually think she was drunk a lot of the time. I know for a fact that in the office upstairs, she kept gin and whiskey in the desk, and she would lock herself in the office and not want to be disturbed.

When I was in the office, you could always see her bottles.

Just down from the office in the hallway upstairs, there used to be a radiator in a recess in the wall. There was just enough room to fit in behind it, down the back, and I used to go there and sit for hours to keep out of her way.

Years later, in my fifties, I told my brother about it, and he said he used to do the same thing, but we never bumped into each other doing it at the same time, which amazes me.

That solitude became a huge part of my life, and even now, I can only last in a room full of friends or people for a short time before I go upstairs to be by myself. I have done this all my life, and it caused lots of arguments with my ex-girlfriends because I never told them about my past or the abuse.

There would be times, like at Christmas or during family meals, when I would disappear to my room, and they would think I was being rude and ignoring their family. But that wasn't the case at all - I would get overwhelmed really quickly and need to get away for a while. At that earlier

stage in my life, I never talked about v
to me as a child - it was a no-go subje
a lot of arguments about my being rude w
was my go-to safety mechanism to survive.

We are hardwired in trauma to find survival stra
that's what helps us get through life, and that never leave
us. That's the way our brains are formed, and that's what
we do to survive. Now, all my friends and family know, and
it's always been a running joke that I would last about
thirty minutes before I'd disappear to be alone. I am
getting better, as I have begun to realise why I do it. Self-
isolation is a part of CPTSD, and like I said, it's my way of
feeling safe and secure.

As I mentioned earlier, I had a terrible fear of the dark
at the time, and Mrs Nobody knew this and used it to instil
fear and terror in me. I'd rather have been slapped in the
face repeatedly by her than be put somewhere dark.
Depending on her mood, she would send me to one of
three places for hours on end if she thought I had broken
one of her rules.

The first place, and the easiest for me, was the laundry
cupboard. I used to climb up the three shelves and fit
between all the towels, staring at the walls for hours on
end until I was allowed out.

The second place was worse: the cupboard under the
stairs, where they kept the hoover, cleaning supplies, and
old Christmas decorations in boxes at the back. It was
worse because it was pitch black - no light at all - but at
least in my mind, it was clean, though dark.

The place I hated the most and would do anything to avoid was the cupboard in the back of the laundry room. It was small and cramped. It was where they kept the bags of potatoes for the home and some garden tools on the wall, as well as the coal for the fires. I hated it because there were loads of cobwebs, nowhere to sit down, and it was pitch black - you couldn't see your hand in front of your face.

I would be terrified because there were spiders and other things on the walls. Even now, I could draw every inch of that place, as it's burned into my memory.

The moment from there being light to the door shutting, bringing complete darkness, in that few seconds, my brain took in every inch of that place, so I knew in the dark what had been there in the light. Depending on her mood or how much she had drunk, she would determine how long I'd stay there - sometimes multiple hours, until bedtime.

My brother and I hadn't talked much about all this, nor had we discussed it with my sister Kath, or *Toots*, as she was known. It was a no-go kind of subject, a strange kind of unspoken understanding - we knew what each of us was going through, but somehow, we knew not to bring it up.

When we did talk, my brother told me that he was passing the outdoor coal bunker one day, which was small, and he heard me inside. The latch had been locked, so he broke it off and found me inside the pitch-black, cramped coal bunker. I have no idea how long I had been in there.

Andrew said there was a lot I had blocked out and forgotten, and in a way, I'm glad, because what I can remember is more than enough for anyone to have in the back of their minds all day, every day.

Another of her favourites was to come in the middle of the night, make up some nonsense about something I had done wrong, and make me go halfway down the stairs onto the little landing. I hated it because you couldn't see around the corner to the bottom of the stairs, and it was pitch black. This was in the 70s, so it was freezing cold as there was no heating in the hallway. She would go back to bed and just leave me there with my fear of the dark and the dread of what lurked at the foot of the stairs. I would sit for hours in the freezing silence, every creak fuelling my terror.

Sometimes, she would leave me there until morning, when I hadn't slept at all, and then I'd be sent to school, where I was supposed to be a model pupil and learn my sums or whatever. What a joke.

I look back now at my report cards saying, "Donald doesn't concentrate or apply himself," and think, if only they knew the reason why. But of course, they didn't.

We had no hope of excelling at school - it was an escape from the crap we had to deal with at the home with Mrs Nobody. We were just glad to be away for those few hours, to try to be ourselves during those brief hours of respite.

Me and my brother Andrew

Me in a school picture

CHAPTER 3:
A DARK TIME

At the time they thought I had hearing problems at school, so I was sent to get my ears tested. The same happened to my sister Kathleen - they tested her hearing because they thought she was partially deaf, which wasn't the case. I was then sent down to Inverness to have a grommet put in my ears, which never helped. Mrs Nobody insisted on driving me, and strangely, on the way back, she bought me a toy – a small German car from the war. What makes it so unusual is that she would never show any kind of kindness to any of us kids, so I'm not sure why she did this.

The operation on my ear didn't help, my attention never improved, nor did my hearing.

My sister Kath had trained herself not to listen to people so she wouldn't give the wrong answer back - strange what you do to survive abuse.

One time we were away at a caravan near Bettyhill, in the far north of Scotland. It was freezing outside - one of those Highland days in April where there was still some snow about - and Mrs Nobody put us out in the bitter cold with just shorts and T-shirts on for hours. I was so cold I could hardly speak, so I knocked on one of the other members of staff's caravans. They took me in, and when Mrs Nobody couldn't find me, the staff member told me to hide in the washing basket. She piled old clothes on top of me and told me to keep still and say nothing.

The caravan door was banged on, and I could hear Mrs Nobody say, "Have you seen Donald? He's nowhere to be seen."

The staff member covered for me, saying I'd just gone over the hill. When Mrs Nobody left, she took me out and told me to go round the back of the caravan. I know now that she was protecting me and probably had a good idea what Mrs Nobody was like. But this was the 70s - it's not like today, with all the systems in place to protect kids. Back then, there was a wall of silence, and if you spoke out, you'd lose your job, and no one would listen or take what you said seriously.

The strange thing was, a few kids would wet the bed out of pure fear, but they would then be ridiculed and beaten by Mrs Nobody, or have the wet sheets rubbed in their faces in front of other kids - anything to make you feel subhuman.

One day, my brother Andrew and I were out in the garden playing. There was a crab apple tree, and Andrew was trying to knock some of the apples off the branches. He grabbed Rusty's bone, to try to knock one down, but he missed, and it hit the window, smashing it and landing on the dinner table.

The next thing we knew, Mrs Nobody was screaming out the window for us to come inside immediately, which we hurried to do out of fear of what was going to happen if we delayed. She took us into the TV room, which was next door to the dining room where we all ate, and she grabbed us, pinning us against the wall.

She was like a rabid dog, screaming and snarling, "Who threw the bone? Who threw the bone?" On and on, like a broken, angry record.

Both Andrew and I stayed completely silent. She took a couple of steps back, then suddenly lunged forward and struck me across the face with full force, sending my head crashing against the wall.

The sound was deafening - a sharp, explosive crack that made everything close in around me. My vision darkened at the edges, as if I were looking through a pair of narrow straws.

I burst into tears - I was only six or seven at the time. Then she turned and hit my brother with the same vicious energy. He fell back but didn't make a sound. He just stared at her with pure hatred and defiance in his eyes, daring her to try and break him.

Then she turned back to me and delivered another blow to the opposite side of my face. The heat from the first was still burning, and now both cheeks throbbed with pain, a red imprint already blooming on my skin.

I was howling.

She lashed out again and again, her voice rising with every blow as she screamed, "Who threw it?"

We stayed silent.

After five or six strikes, I couldn't breathe, couldn't speak - I was shaking uncontrollably. I now realise I was having my first ever panic attack. It was the beginning of something I'd go on to battle all my life. I genuinely thought I was going to die.

Once she had exhausted her rage, realising we wouldn't betray each other, she finally sent us to our rooms.

That moment, I now realise, was pivotal in my life - the kind that changes everything, leaving a permanent mark. My brother and I knew this wouldn't be the end of it, but we were powerless to do anything. And that fear was a powerful tool to keep people silent.

People throughout my life have asked, "Why didn't you tell anyone?" And the truth is we saw what happened to the other kids if they tried to tell their parents when they visited - they would get the shit beaten out of them, and they wouldn't try it twice. So that was it for us. That was our life - be invisible, be silent, and learn the ways to keep yourself as safe as you could.

The damage Mrs Nobody caused to so many kids is breathtaking. I know of kids who grew up with serious mental health issues, and as I said, drink and drug problems. Many had suicidal thoughts for years, and I know of a few who are not here today - they found life too hard.

She was meant to be caring for us, as many of the kids had come from horrendous family situations, only to be put in that monster. She's dead now and no one seems to care what she did, no one takes responsibility, and no one wants it mentioned.

Eventually her reign of terror came to an end. She was carrying a large pan of boiling water and fell over, scalding her whole body. My last memory of her was lying on the kitchen floor, scalded, before the ambulance came and took her away. It may sound callous but we were all over the moon when we heard she was never coming back – and I never saw her again.

My brother saw her a few years later after he had left the children's home. She was on the other side of the road with a walking stick. He never confronted her, as she was old and frail - he just left her to it.

I often wonder what I would do if I could see her today and explain to her the damage she caused to so many people, but I don't think she would care. So, to me, she's a sad memory that I don't waste time thinking about any more. Our brains have many ways to cope with horrible memories, and everyone deals with it differently. I've spoken to a lot of the kids who grew up in the children's home at that time, and they have their own stories to tell about their abuse at the hands of Mrs Nobody. They tend not to tell anyone what happened to them, and some I have spoken to have said that I'm the first person they've talked to about what happened. I think it's easier because I was there, and they don't feel the need to prove what they're saying. They also understand that I went through it too.

I was the same - I was a total closed book - it wasn't for discussion. But these things come back to haunt you, no matter how strong you think you are. And when you least expect it - boom - it's triggered, and you go into meltdown, and your life starts to fall apart through no conscious choice of your own. Your body never forgets.

I often think no one understands the devastating effect childhood abuse has on a person's life and development - it's like a grenade goes off in your brain, and nothing will ever be the same.

I find it breathtaking, the lack of accountability, as now, many years on, the victims are only just coming forward from their silence, fifty or so years later, as they realise how unjust it was. Like I said, many came from abusive situations, only to suffer worse abuse from the person or people meant to care for them. And as in many cases, the person doing the abuse is dead, so there's not much justice or desire to find out the truth from any authorities.

Many people I grew up with have told me they've never even told their partners about what happened, even though their partners could sense something traumatic had happened to them at some point. Some can't even bring themselves to think about it, as the memories are too painful. I myself had put this all in a dark place at the back of my mind until I was forty-two, but as I was to find out, your brain and body will only allow you so long before it forces you to address what happened, and to ignore that at your own peril. As the famous book says, *The Body Keeps the Score*.

Things improved a lot after Mrs Nobody removed herself from our lives, and we got on with living a more normal life - well, as normal as a children's home could be. The new lady who took over was Christine Ross, who later married and became Christine Grey. She was kind, patient, and treated the kids as if they were special to her - what a change from the earlier start to my life. My sister Christine had moved out at some point to start her life, and she lived not far from the home, just a few streets away really, and I used to go visit her a lot. She would have crisps and cola for me, and it was great to visit. She would also always buy me the latest edition of the Guinness Book of Records. I became obsessed with learning facts at this time and would read it from cover to cover, reciting various world records to anyone who would listen. Learning has stuck with me all my life, and I study loads of esoteric things that my brain finds fascinating.

During this time, we were given a class project to do that would culminate in giving a talk to our class on any chosen subject, and mine was on UFOs or unidentified flying objects. Now, don't ask me why, but I became obsessed with that subject from the age of seven, and it's stuck with me to this day. Every day, I study the subject and can recite almost any case off by heart. I also became obsessed with the universe and later in life, quantum science - in fact, anything unusual about what it means to be a human being.

In the home, they had a rota of staff who worked 2pm through till 2pm the next day and they slept over in staff bedroom, and for the most part, I got on great with the staff. They were kind and caring and tried their best to make life enjoyable for us kids. At the time, my best friend was Donnie Murray. He had been in the children's home with me for a while when he was young, then moved just down the road to stay with his granny and grandad. Their family was like a second family to me, and I would be down there every single day - we were inseparable. If I wasn't at his, he was up at the home with me.

We used to go off on some mad adventures and we would often be out from morning till night. We used to go out hunting for treasures at the back of the garages at the children's home, where people would dump car parts and anything else. A lot of times, we would find a bag of porno magazines, which we found funny as we were only kids. We were always together, and Donnie's family was like my family.

At this time, a lot of the kids in the home would spend most of their time with each other. There were some characters and some mad things going on. One day, a kid in the home with us told us he planned to jump the garages at the back of the children's home - his name was Neil. Now, bear in mind the garage was about nine feet high and long enough to hold a car. My brother and I didn't fancy his chances, but Neil was adamant that it could be done. After a while, he got some blocks and a sheet of wood that had been around the back of the children's home and set up a ramp. Instantly, my brother and I could see the problem - it only came to about two feet off the ground. We tried to point this out, but Neil was having none of it, so my brother said, "Yeah, okay then, if you're so sure, go for it." So, Neil goes to the top of the hill, comes flying down, up the ramp at full speed, and hits the garage door , landing in a heap on the ground with a burst nose. He got up, shocked that he never made it.

Luckily, he was okay, but my brother and I found it hilarious. Apart from some bruises and a burst nose, he was fine. That was the kind of daily crazy stuff that went on.

Donnie, my brother, and a kid called PD used to play this game where PD, who lived in the home with us, always had air rifles and pistols. We would go across the road to the big cattle mart that used to be across from the home, and we would shoot targets, etc. But we also played a game where we would get our big parka coats, zip them right up, and then someone would shoot the air gun at your wellies. Beyond stupid, I know, but that was the game we played.

One day, it was my brother's turn to shoot the air rifle, and PD jumped out a bit too close to him. The pellet, which normally didn't do much at range, went through his jeans and hit him in the butt cheek. He pulled down his jeans, and there was this little dent with a small trickle of blood coming from it. He was okay, but again, this was the foolish shit we used to get up to every day.

I never had a sense of danger and would always be doing stupid things that could have easily killed me. One time, when roller skates were all the rage, I decided I could skate from the top of Rose Street to the bottom - it's a steep hill with junctions for cars coming out. Well, I didn't get far before crashing and taking loads of skin off my back, to the point that I had to sleep on my front for a couple of weeks. Looking back, it was beyond stupid, but risk-taking is a known part of CPTSD. Like I said, it sways your life from deep in your brain - you are not in control of your risk-taking.

Other things we used to do included climbing on top of high buildings' roofs or jumping off the top of garages. If it was dangerous, we were doing it. I was with Donnie one time in an industrial yard, climbing this oil tank up against a cliff face, and I fell off it, dropping about ten feet. Luckily, I landed between the wall and the tank. If I had missed, I wouldn't be writing this book right now as there another huge drop beyond the wee ledge I luckily landed on. I also used to climb the cliffs in Thurso at a fast pace, with no fear of falling, and I almost did on a few occasions. Now, bearing in mind that a few people have lost their lives on those exact same cliffs, I look back and realise why I was taking risks. It's a strange thing when we look at pieces of our lives with an older brain. Sometimes I get a shiver down my spine when I think of the things we were doing - beyond dangerous.

I didn't always come away unscathed. One day I was way up the river with a good pal, Ronnie Gray, and we decided to move this big, massive slab of concrete we had found. He got one end, and I got the other. For some reason, he lost his grip on it, and it fell out of his hands, ripping it out of mine, and fell on my ankle, badly fracturing it.

Ronald looked at my ankle, sticking up at an unnatural angle, and he panicked and ran off – understandably freaked out. So, I had to crawl all the way back along the path, then up a super steep hill, before my pal's dad found me crawling home. He put me on his bike and wheeled me home. I was on crutches all that summer, and for someone like me, with unlimited energy and always climbing tall things, it was a reminder that there was a price to reckless behaviour - but my brain couldn't register that.

Donnie Murray and me aged ten,
me with the most ill fitting shorts ever

Me aged nine engrossed in the guiness
book of records at my sister christine house

CHAPTER 4:

SAME ROOM, WRONG BED

Over the years, social workers made several attempts to find foster homes for both my brother Andrew and my sister Kathleen. For my brother, it was actually an American couple, but he hated it and had a deep mistrust of people, to the point where he flatly refused to go. As for my sister Kathleen, she was sent to a family home, and I will call the woman *Mrs Clog*.

Our dog Rusty, whom I totally adored, died when I was around nine years this had a huge impact on me as I loved Rusty unconditionally and for me at that age the love back from Rusty meant the world to me the worst part was he passed away on April 1st. I came home from school at lunchtime, and they told me Rusty had passed away.

I said, "Ah, April Fool's," but unfortunately, it was true - it was terrible timing landing on that day. I was beyond broken by Rusty's passing.

Rusty had given me unconditional love as a kid, and all the children adored him. I was so distraught that I had to be sent home from school the next day. It was another one of those cruel kicks in the teeth that life seems to serve up, that he died on April Fool's Day.

I look back now and think, "Wow, how stupid all the things we used to get up to were," but at the time, it was just normal. Those times were magical, always an adventure, and the stupid stuff we did was breathtaking. If it was high and dangerous, Donnie and I climbed it. We would go miles up the river with tractor inner tubes we'd get from the tyre centre, build a raft on them, and float down the river for miles until we got to the harbour in Thurso.

Donnie understood me, and he had seen some of the same things himself. He and his brother and sisters hadn't had the easiest starts in life either, but we all understood each other, so I never had to explain or talk about it, which made things easier. However, it wasn't all fun and easy times - it never is in a children's home in the 70s. Depending on how many kids were in the home, sometimes you would have to change bedrooms, etc.

At this time when I was about seven, I was put in a room with an older girl - I will call her *Kelly* for now - she was maybe fourteen or so but I was made to share with her. Late one night she came from her bed and started to climb into mine whilst I was asleep. I woke up to find her on top of me with a nightgown on but nothing underneath. My pyjama bottoms were pulled down. She then put her mouth over my mouth and was trying to kiss me.

All I recall was her hot breath on my face. It's something that stuck with me all my life, she then started rubbing and grinding up and down me and I just lay there still. I was silent and motionless As she climbed on top of me and did what she wanted to do

After what seemed like ages she got off me went back to her bed and behaved like nothing happened. This went on every night like a routine.

I would try to stay awake, but she would wait till I fell asleep. Then I would wake with her either getting in my bed or grinding on top of me. Even today the slightest sound in my house causes me to wake up startled, ready for war. It never leaves us, all those nights of trying to stay awake to prevent the abuse. It has always stayed with me.

I never ever told the staff, as by now we were well versed in keeping quiet. And as weird as it may seem - in the scale of things, and what I had been through - this wasn't the worst thing to happen.

I know that sounds messed up but that's just the truth.

I did tell a couple of boys that were older, but they just found it funny and laughed. That's just the way it was. I have found it weird when someone says what age did you lose your virginity - my brain is always like, *Do I tell them it was around six or seven or do I tell them I was thirteen?* Although 13 is young as well, at least that time it was by my choice.

Eventually she was moved out of the children's home down south with her family and I was left to try and process what happened I had no concept of sex or abuse so my brain just didn't understand what had happened to me another thing to add to the messed up shit I would have to process later in life and deal with the images in my head just one more fucked up thing to add to the messed up list.

Now, she was not the only one, but there are things I won't talk about, even in this book. Sometimes, the memories we have are just too painful to think about, let alone discuss. But I am trying to deal with some dark things, and in time I will process a lot of the messed-up shit I have seen in my life. I have spoken to others who also have traumatic memories of what happened back then, and I know exactly what they're talking about.

I thought long and hard about including this in the book. It's incredibly difficult to talk about the dark things that have broken you, but I want to be as honest as my brain will allow. Shame and guilt are powerful emotions. Ultimately, I concluded that these experiences are an important part of what shaped who I am and how I think. Sometimes, things just need to be said—yet sometimes, they remain simply too painful.

I remind myself that there were many kids in the home who had endured even worse and more unfair treatment from their own families before they even arrived. We would hear about these horrors in graphic detail. Those were the conversations we had, even as adults, and they were heartbreaking. How on earth were we meant to process all that as kids?

When kids have a normal family life, when they speak to their siblings, they talk about normal stuff. When we kids talked, it was about why their dad raped them, or why their mum and dad couldn't look after them because they were drunk all the time, or how they were neglected in some way. Those were the conversations we had, and guess what - to us, it was completely normal. Only now do

I realise how messed up it was, but that's life in a children's home.

School, at this point, was pretty good. I had a lot of good friends from my class, and I used to socialise with them outside of school as well. Paul, who lived down the road from me, I used to go down most Saturdays and hang out with him. His mum was my PE teacher at school, and she and her family were really kind to me. I found out years later that she had planned to adopt me, but in the end, due to my bond with my brother, they decided not to split us up. We had many great times together, and I'm grateful for their kindness.

Also, Shaun, who lived just up the road - his mum and dad were so much fun. They would put on gaming parties for their sons' birthdays, which I would attend. We would play snooker and darts and win prizes - a brilliant family who were also really kind to me.

By that time, life in the children's home was pretty good, thanks to Christine and the rest of the staff.

Tommy and I were still playing pranks or getting into some kind of mischief that would result in us either getting the belt at school or being grounded. One day, it was school sports day, and Tommy and I were up at the sandpit where the long jump was going to be. I persuaded Tommy to piss in the sandpit, and after some persuasion, he agreed.

As soon as we got back to class, I said, "Miss, Tommy did a pish in the sandpit!"

The look on Tommy's face was priceless - he got detention, and I thought it was hilarious. A few days later,

I thought Tommy had forgotten about it and seen the funny side. We were in the toilets at the urinals talking, and then Tommy suddenly turned round and pissed all over my leg. That was the way it was back then - funny laughs. We were inseparable at school, and again, I never discussed any of the stuff that happened to me - it was locked away.

A strange thing in our school - bear in mind this was the seventies - was that if you had anything different about you, that became your nickname. For example, there was Luggsy because he had big ears, or Crack Eye because he had a squint eye, or Dougie Specks because he wore glasses. It didn't matter what it was - if something was different, that became your nickname. I had freckles, so I got called Freckle Face sometimes.

At the time, my music teacher discovered I had an amazing singing voice and started entering me into the local music festivals. I won every time, getting the highest marks with distinctions, and I still have all the certificates. That all stopped when I hit puberty though, and my voice dropped - now my singing is awful!

I enjoyed my time at Miller Academy. I made great pals, and life wasn't too crazy, as by then, the home was a good place to live, and the staff were really kind and caring to us. You still had the daily threats of pissing off one of the older kids who wouldn't be afraid to give you a beating – you had to be vigilant, always on guard, but at the same time, you got on with living life.

I was really close to Christine, and I saw her as my mother figure. Her family was also amazing to us - her dad Rosser was well-known in Thurso, as he was our local postie, and we would help him with his rounds to the houses around the children's home. He would give us money for sweets - he was just one of life's great human beings, as was all of Christine's family. They would always do kind things for us. Christine would take us to see her family from time to time, and I loved it, as they showed me great kindness. Christine's sister Bettine would cut our hair. I laughed, as one time, another kid and I locked ourselves in the bathroom with a pair of scissors and cut our own hair - you can imagine what that looked like! Bettine had to salvage what was left and make it look presentable. I felt blessed to have known Christine's mum and dad and extended family, as they showed me what great humans were actually like.

As time went on, my pal Donnie told me about a dance he had seen. I was twelve years old at this point, and he had also started learning it. I asked, "What kind of dance?" and he showed me what I later learned was breakdancing. He showed me an arm wave from body popping

This was the first time I'd ever seen anything like that, and I was gobsmacked - how was that possible? He looked double-jointed!

At the time, in Thurso, many of our friends were American, as there were a lot of US service families staying there. They had an area where all the Americans lived, and a street called John Kennedy Drive. We loved it up there, as it was so different from our lives in Thurso. The people were different, the houses looked different, the cars were poles apart, and even the swing park was completely unusual.

I had a good pal called Gary who lived up there, so I would hang out around the park with the American kids. There were two guys called Melvin and Ruben - one African American and the other Filipino - and one day, Melvin started body popping. My jaw hit the floor - you see, it's not like now, where you know what breakdancing and body popping look like. I had no reference - it just blew my mind. He looked like a super fluent robot, and sometimes like he had no joints. I was shocked - how was this possible for a human to move like this? I was determined to learn.

Donnie told me that a good friend of ours, Graham Scanlon, was good at body popping, so I eventually caught up with him and was really impressed with his dancing. Also, at the time, I had been working on balancing on one hand with my elbow in my belly and had started turning it into a hand spin. Every day, I would practice and learn a couple of new moves. Since I was young, I had always gone to Thurso Youth Club, and as I was getting older, we used to go there and practice our breakdancing. That's where I mastered a back somersault. We would practice every youth club night on our moves. Helen, the leader there, used to encourage us and let us use the place to train.

The youth club allowed us to get really good at breakdancing, and at the same time, we had many laughs there.

After a while, I got to know a lot more guys who were breakdancing. I heard a guy called Donnie Williamson had started a class down in the local Boys' Brigade hall, so I went along. He was a great body popper, amazing with arm waves, and good at robotics. I learned a lot from him about popping and locking. By then, it was getting popular. A good pal from school, Robbie Bell, had been dancing, and we hooked up with another pal, Willie Miller. We also hooked up with Iain and Ali Elder, as well as Cooter and a few others.

Just as this was happening, around 1982 or 83, we were told the Thurso children's home was shutting, and they were moving us all through to Wick. Just as life was getting stable, with a good home life and a good circle of friends who I was really close to, they decided to uproot us all and move us twenty miles away from all my friends.

I was devastated, as it meant leaving my high school, where all my pals were, and going to Wick High.

I had no choice in the matter though. I was uprooted from the only solid things I had in my life and moved to a brand-new town where I didn't really know anyone. How many kicks to the teeth and letdowns was I supposed to endure in life? Another gut-wrenching thing to endure, and I just had to shut up about it. This was a major upheaval for me, and my anxiety went through the roof, but the decision had been made.

It was a tough move - I was gutted. The new children's home was more like a centre than a home, very clinical and not much like a family home, which the Thurso children's home had become through the love and passion of Christine and the other staff members who worked so hard to improve our lives. I couldn't seem to catch a break in life - all the stability was gone. My breakdance pals had become like family; we were all really tight. I didn't have to explain anything to them about who I was or my messed-up past - they accepted me for me, and that was a very powerful form of acceptance.

I put a brave face on it, as I had no other choice. After a few weeks, I made some new pals among the breakdancers of Wick, who went on to become great friends. The breakdancers knew I lived in a children's centre, but they never really pried or asked too much, and I loved that. I was just one of the boys.

My English teacher from Thurso High was a lovely lady named Mrs Fraser, came through to visit me at the Wick centre. She brought me bags of sweets, a card, and magazines, which meant the world to me. Now, it blows me away how kind she was. She passed away a while ago, and I left a nice comment on a Facebook post about it. Her daughter messaged me to say that I had really touched her mum's heart and that her mum would talk about me from time to time. When I read the message, I burst out crying. I think about Mrs Fraser from time to time with a big smile, and I feel blessed to have known her - her kindness was beautiful, one of life's beautiful souls that we meet on our journey.

Some of my best pals from the Wick side were Gordie Green, Lee Fleming and his brother Michael, Rusty and Bruce Ewing, Sharkey, Terry Johnston, and Hammy. All the lads were great - we were all really tight and saw each other almost every day at school and then at Wick Youth Club, which we went to almost every night. They would have a disco most weekends where we would go and hit the floor with our latest moves to impress the girls and compete - or battle, as it's called in breakdancing - to see who was *'top dog'*. They were some really talented dancers and some of the best people to grow up with.

Me, teaching myself windmills

My breakdance crew - The Egyption Warriors at a competition

Top left Willie Miller, top right Robbie Bell.
Bottom left to right Donnie Williamson, Ali Elder and myself

CHAPTER 5:

UPHEAVAL AND BREAKDANCING

It's strange - there was always a rivalry between Wick and Thurso people, but all the breakdancers were pals. I used to see all my Wick breakdance pals during the week and then later see all my Thurso breakdance pals at the weekend. It was a workable routine but came with lots of problems, as Thurso was twenty miles away, and I wanted to spend all my time there. My pals' mums were brilliant with me - I used to either stay at my good pal Willie Miller's house, where his mum Joan Miller and his dad were brilliant, letting me stay there most weekends and feeding me. There was also Iain and Ali Elder's mum, Joan Elder, who would let me stay there loads too. Both would feed me and make sure everything was smoothed over with the children's centre in Wick, ensuring I was okay to stay there and that they would look after me and make sure I didn't get into any trouble. I owe them a lot - they made my life immeasurably better.

Funny thing is, sometimes there would be ten or so kids in Ali and Iain's house, and we would watch *Breakdance the Movie* on the VHS machine, then get one of Joan's old album covers out to do head spins in her living room, routinely kicking her ornaments off the sideboard or crashing into it. On Sunday nights, I had to get back to the Wick children's centre, and I used to take the bus that took people through to Wick Hospital. I never had any money, but you just had to make a donation, and I would have to find something to put in the tin. Joan Elder made sure that before I headed back to Wick, I would have Sunday dinner with them - a big roast chicken with all the extras, and trifle. She was so good to all us kids taking over her home at the weekend - brilliant memories.

It was the same at Willie Millar's - Willie had some lino in his room, and we would go up and practise all the time. It's amazing the moves we did in that small room - great times.

To save the little money I got, I quite often would just thumb a lift from Wick to Thurso so I could keep the bus fare for spending. On more than one occasion, I had to walk pretty much the whole way, but overall, I used to get lifts all the time without telling the children's centre people. I loved spending time in Thurso - it was my home, and I loved spending time with my Wick breakdance pals. It was all about acceptance and family.

Over time, I wanted to spend more and more time with my Thurso pals. We had started a breakdance team called the Egyptian Warriors, and by then, we were going to competitions almost every couple of weeks. We would win almost every single comp - we only ever lost one, which we all say was a fix! Going to the comps were the best times ever, and we would always be practising for hours upon hours on the streets with a piece of cardboard or lino, or in Ali and Iain's house or Willie Millar's house, as he had a great bit of lino in his room. We would polish it to death and practise head spins. We practised so many head spins that the hair on the tops of our heads started to wear out, and we all had these little egg-shaped bald spots on top of our heads. Sometimes, our heads would bleed from the sheer number of head spins, but we were driven and intent on being the best.

At the time, we were in a Wick dance school, Carols School of Dance, and going to the competitions was brilliant fun. All the disco dancers had the front of the bus, and the breakdancers had the back. There were people who would sneak vodka or beers on the bus, and we would have a laugh all the way down with all the disco dancers and mums who went with us. There was always some madness going on at the back of the bus, and you can bet us breakdancers were in the midst of it.

We eventually went on to become the Scottish Breakdance Crew Champions after winning all the heats before the grand finals in Glasgow's Zanzibar nightclub. We got a lot of recognition for this - we were on the radio and had our picture in the local paper. We were also sponsored at the time by Jim Bews Video Shop, which was local in Thurso, and he provided us with our team tracksuits and trainers.

By then, though, the Wick children's centre was giving me a really hard time. I would ask them for some money to go to the competitions, and they would give me grief, as they obviously had a small budget for each kid. At the time,

I couldn't understand, as all I wanted to do was enter with my team and win, but now I totally get it. I had become obsessed with being the best and would practise at least three or four hours every day. When I would leave my Thurso pals, the next time I saw them the following week, I would have five new moves or would have mastered a particular move. I always had that single-minded dedication where I would train for hours upon hours. It was like I was driven from deep down to climb out of the shitty start I had in life. I guess I had to prove I was somebody and that I wasn't just an afterthought in life. I also loved the respect of being one of the best and the attention from girls and peers alike - it made me feel like, finally, I wasn't a nobody. I had been told so many times as a kid that no one loved me, I was unwanted, I was just a stupid orphan. If you're told that every day from a young age, it affects you. Breakdancing and going to comps allowed me to stand out from the crowd, to be somebody, and to be the best. We used to call it being a "ghetto celebrity" - you were a nobody, but to those who knew you, you were a somebody.

At this time, I had been having problems at school - arguments with teachers and authority figures. I had been given the belt more times than I can remember, and I didn't care. I started bunking off Wick High School and thumbing a lift to Thurso so I could hang out with my pals at Thurso High. I even used to pretend to be other people just to go to class for a laugh. Sometimes, I'd wake up in the morning, and on the days, I didn't head to Thurso, I would hang out with the Fleming brothers, as they lived round the corner from me, and Michael would write sick notes for school for me. But by then, my attendance had become really bad, and the school had notified the children's centre, who then tried to stop me from going to Thurso to see my pals or to go to dancing.

I look back at this time and understand it from both viewpoints, but the thing was, I already had so much resentment from being moved from my pals, and hidden trauma I had internalised to the point where I didn't even think about it. This culminated in my having a physical confrontation with a teacher at school. He used to always slag off breakdancing to me and my pals, and after class one day, I got detention. He had told me breakdancing was crap and that I was never going to get anywhere with it. I told him he was a dick and to shut his mouth. The criticism from him brought me right back to Mrs Nobody, and boom - my back was up. He then made the mistake of trying to pin me against the wall by the neck. Bad move - it was on. Anytime anyone got in my face, I reacted badly. All the memories of the past would overtake me, and I would explode.

Anyway, this added to an already broken situation. The school phoned the children's centre and gave them their bullshit explanation, but they later found out the truth, and I was allowed back to school - not that I even cared. I was banned by the staff at the children's centre from seeing my friends, travelling to Thurso at the weekends, or attending any breakdance comps for a minimum of six weeks. I lasted about two days before I was thumbing it back to Thurso to see my mates. I think after a couple of weeks, they realised this wasn't going to work, and a compromise was worked out.

It's funny years later, I got a copy of the notes that the children's centre had made on me at the time, and their lack of understanding of who I was or how hard it was to leave everything I needed in life was breathtaking. I laughed when I read the amount of bullshit in it to try and make me look really bad - a lot of it was made up, I might add. The staff members who had come from the Thurso children's home understood me better, and Christine Gray was always there for me. She was the closest person I had in life to a mum, and one of the last messages I sent to her was telling her that, and I'm eternally grateful that I did. She used to let me stay at her house on the weekends, which was so kind of her - she and her husband Ally were the best towards me, showing such amazing kindness. As I said, she was an amazing influence on me, and I kept in close contact with her throughout the years. I owe her so much a lot of who I became was down to her bringing me up with a great sense of kindness and love, and I feel blessed to have had her in my life.

Now, I know I was not easy - would you be, living my life? But I was kind to the people around me, to the other kids, even though I came with issues. I always said, try doing one week of my life back then, and you would understand.

Going to Thurso and being with my pals was the only time I felt really normal and accepted. Nothing and no one were going to take that away from me. While the centre staff thought I was just acting out and being a little shit, they never understood it from my point of view. How could they? We were never going to see eye to eye on this, and for me, it was not up for debate. I had gone through enough bullshit - I just wanted a normal life with my pals.

All my breakdance pals accepted me unconditionally, and that was a really powerful thing. They were all there for me when I needed them - no explanations needed. At this time, I was living life to the max. We used to hang out up at John Kennedy Drive with all the Americans. One of the girls who used to hang out with us was a girl named Kerry H. Her mum was a single parent and used to work night shifts at the local American air base, so the house was free on the weekends. Me and all my Thurso breakdance pals would go and stay there and party. There were loads of girls, drink, and madness going on, and we lived it to the max. Every weekend, we would be hanging out with girls and practising how many backflips we could do at the boating pond or putting green. There was usually a competition to see who could do the most. By then, we had taught ourselves to do back somersaults off buildings, so there was an ongoing challenge to see who could do it off the highest thing - like climbing frames, school sheds, or the stage at school as the kids walked around - or who could do the most backflips in a row. It was mostly about bragging rights, but it was also friendly and about pushing each other to be the best. We had no fear.

There were always kids who were jealous of the attention we got, or they used to say breakdancing was gay, but we took no shit from anyone. There was often a fight here or there, but we didn't care. There was almost consistent madness going on, like one night we were all at Willie Millar's house, and there was a barn dance on at Halkirk that we wanted to go to. At the time, we all had the skunk hairstyle, called the skunk because it was dyed black on the sides and the top was pure white. Donnie wanted his hair streaked before we went, but we didn't have much time, so Willie put the cap on his head and pulled his hair through the holes - no easy task, as Donnie had really curly hair back then. We put the hair dye on his head, and to speed it up, we used two packs. Time was catching up, so Willie borrowed his sister's hairdryer to help speed up the process. It was still taking too long, so we got a second hairdryer and proceeded to heat Donnie's hair up, then - boom - his hair burst into flames! He got up in a panic, jumping around like a human candle. He ran to the bedroom, we chased after him, then grabbed him and quickly pulled him to the bathroom, where we stuck his head under the tap and extinguished the flames. Luckily, he was unhurt, as he had really thick, bushy hair, but the cap was like melted cheese when we pulled it off. But surprisingly, he looked fine, with no injuries, and off we went to the barn dance. That was just a typical weekend for us.

Donnie was always up to insane stuff, like the time up at the Elders' house when he started fixing an old TV and stuck a non-grounded screwdriver in the back to see what would happen. Bang! Donnie went flying after electrocuting himself. He was fine, but that was just another one of those cracked events. To me, all that mattered was spending time with my pals and practising breakdancing to try and make a better life for myself. Actually, one of the teachers in Wick used to say to me, "Right, Mackenzie, are you going to do any work today?" And I'd say, "Probably not." He used to make a deal with me - if I did the work, he would then let me go to the back of the class and practise my moves, which I loved. He even got a massive bit of lino for me when the school was changing the flooring - really heavy-duty lino for me to take home to train on. Top teacher. I met him a few years later when we were doing a Kuk Sool demo, and he said he always knew I would do something with my life. That has stuck with me even to today - there are many different roads to success in life.

After a while, I started to adjust to life in the Wick centre, but I found it tough. I now know I was struggling badly with life events and started to really rebel against everything. I'd spend as much time as I could at my pals' houses. A really close friend who was also a breakdancer from Wick was called Gordie Green, and we just seemed to click - we were like brothers. I was always around his house. He had a few sisters, and we had a laugh whenever I was there, looking out for each other. We were closer than brothers and often got up to mad adventures. It's hard enough as a teen anyway, and I think I was struggling deep within, trying to find my place in the bigger scheme of things. Like I said, I never confided in my friends or talked about my past—it was a no-go area—but somehow, although ever-present, I managed to contain it, or so I thought.

There were always kids coming and going in the children's home and children's centre, so you never got really close to anyone, but at the same time, you were closer to each other because you understood and realised that the kids around you had messed-up lives and trauma of their own to deal with. We kind of looked out for each other in that way. There was never the money for things that most kids got - there was a budget for kids, from the cost of trainers to the cost of tops - so we never got the kind of stuff or clothes that would make you cool at school. This, in turn, adds a layer of anxiety and stress to a teenage life.

One Christmas they asked me what I wanted, and I said a Nike Windrunner jacket and a portable stereo so I could play music when I was out practising my moves in the park. I knew I wouldn't get that, but they made me tell them what I wanted anyway. Well, on Christmas Day, they bought me an imitation Nike jacket and a radio your granny would have. Now, I neither expected nor got what I wanted, and I was used to that by then, but what was hard was when I went up to my pals in Thurso and they had brand-new stereos, Nike jackets, and trainers, etc. I hid the fake jacket I got - not that my pals would have said anything, but rather just because of the other kids in general. It was just another thing reminding me that I wasn't the same as the rest of my friends - another reminder, and just another disappointment.

Even today, I always feel incredibly awkward if someone buys me a gift, and I will never take anything from anyone. I'm not sure why, but I find it really tough to accept kindness of any sort. I have worked for absolutely everything I have in life - I have been given nothing, nor will I ever accept anything. I feel I should earn everything I have - that way, I owe nothing to anyone in life. That's the way I like it, and that's why I trained harder than anyone else at breakdancing and then in martial arts in later life. I earned it, I owned it, and when I became the best, it also gave me validation and a sense of value that I had lacked for a huge portion of my life. I suppose I felt I was not good enough or was a failure - that had been burned into my mind from Mrs Nobody all those years ago. "No one wants you; no one loves you, you're not worthy, you're useless, everyone hates you, you're a burden, you're stupid, you're thick" - I could fill this book with those words burned into my soul. I was also told by more than one teacher that I was either destined to end up in jail or a total failure in life, but I never listened because deep in my soul, I had a raging fire burning that craved to be someone different from others, but to gain respect and validation from those around me. I was driven in a way that was really hard to .

The warriors winning Scottish teams breakdance champs

Donnie Williamson & I practicing floor freeze at Thurso High School

Egyptian warriors crew 1985

Breakdance comps warriors jamming with a breakdance crew from down south

CHAPTER 6:

BE REALISTIC

Like I said, if there was a move that no one could do, I would go away and practise for hours every day until I had mastered the impossible skills that others couldn't do. And even then, as soon as I mastered that new skill, I would instantly find the next skill I was never satisfied with where I was at.

A friend said to me, "You are always searching for the unsearchable." I would say to myself, "When I achieve this, I'll know I've made it." And as soon as I did that, I would go straight on to the next challenge. I was never satisfied, nor content. I know this will stay with me for the rest of my life. I think I'm trying to prove something to myself, and I'm never happy with the result, no matter how good. It's like a curse, but it's me - it's the way I'm made.

Anyway, even now, I hate Christmas - so do my brother Andrew and my sister Kathleen.

As time went on in the Wick children's centre, I realised that in order to get anywhere, I'd have to forge an extraordinary life. Once, when I went to the careers officer, they sat me down and asked what I wanted to be in life. I said I wanted to be a professional breakdancer. I still remember them bursting out laughing and saying, "A what?" I repeated, "A professional breakdancer." By then, they knew I was serious, and I could see the patronising look they gave me. "How about something a bit more realistic?" they said. "How about a plumber or a bricklayer?" I repeated that I wanted to become a professional breakdancer. I was told that was totally unrealistic and that I needed to get that idea out of my head. Although later in life, I did become a pro breakdancer for many years - I'll talk about that later in the book - back to the career officer.

"Okay, let's try again. If you can't become a breakdancer, what else do you want to become?" they asked. I said, "There is nothing else." They insisted, "If you can't say breakdancer, what else would you choose?" I thought for a while and said, "Martial arts instructor." By then, I had become totally inspired by Bruce Lee and the way no one could touch or harm him. I wanted to be like him - untouchable, invincible. Now, bear in mind we were in the far north of Scotland, where job choices were not like they are in a city, especially not back in 1985. I can see why they might have thought my choices were unrealistic, but to me, I knew I had a burning desire, and nothing and no one was going to stop me. Now, as I look back at age fifty-four, I realise I did both - forty years of martial arts teaching and twenty years as a pro breakdancer. Like I always knew, my destiny was mine and mine alone to shape. Even at a young age, my school reports, which I still have, said, "Donald has far too much imagination and not enough grounding in reality." It's strange, as an adult in your fifties, looking back now - if I were writing the report cards the teacher who wrote that then, I would write, "They need to have more imagination and belief in people and stop basing things on a bland reality." But hey, what do I know? I just know everything I said I was going to do and achieve, I did. My friends will tell you I had a single-minded dedication burning just below the surface, and no - failure in life was not an option. It would have proved Mrs Nobody right, and I'd rather die than let that happen.

Actually, I would love to see her now, just for five minutes, and say, "All your bullshit that you thought would break my soul actually gave me the drive and ambition to create a life that was different, full of achievements, and dedicated to helping change others' lives." One of my personal training clients, years later, would ask me about my life and early years, and I told him a little bit. He was African and very spiritual, in touch with the universe and nature, and one day he said something to me that I found profound. He said, "Don, what if all that abuse was a gift?" At first, I was really offended but kept my mouth shut. After a while, I asked, "What do you mean?" He replied, "If you had not gone through all the abuse and endured those hardships in life, you would never have the understanding and drive to help others now." Wow, I thought, as I usually gave him the motivational talks along with the hard training. That's probably one of the most profound things I have heard. The torture that's in your soul that has caused so much suffering, both physically and mentally - a gift? That took some thinking about. Maybe it's a different cultural thing, but perhaps the abuse - physical, mental, and sexual - all came together to drive my life, which I have dedicated to making a positive change in the hundreds of men, women, and children I have taught over the years or performed breakdancing for. It's a weird concept - something broken fixing so many others. Maybe I will grow to understand that more as I get older.

As I was getting towards sixteen in the Wick children's centre, they were asking me more and more about my future and what I was going to do, as at sixteen, I had to leave the children's centre and start out on my own. One thing I did like in the children's centre was the domestic staff - they were kind to me and looked after me. Fiona, Elaine, and Rena were there to talk or just give me extra chips on my plate, which I loved. For the most part, I had an uneasy truce with most of the new staff that had not come from Ormile Road. Whereas they saw me as rebellious and answering back, they were totally unaware that at this point, I already had pronounced C-PTSD, which I would get diagnosed with later in life. They just saw me as awkward to deal with, but C-PTSD comes with a host of behavioural problems, and I had most of them. I didn't trust anyone, especially people in a position of power over me, as up to that point, it had been a huge struggle just to relate to normal people. My brain was hard-wired to be on edge, distrustful of others, and readying myself for the next disappointment or being verbally attacked, that I was somehow not good enough or that I was a problem.

When I look back, I wish I could have met the me of now, back then, and I would have said, "You don't need validation from anyone in life. These people are deeply flawed, like all humans. Find your courage and strength from within yourself, as no one is coming to save you. You're on your own, but you've got this. You will survive; you will get through this. Have faith." But as a 15-year-old, we don't have the life experience or wisdom to tell ourselves this - it's something we only earn over time. It's one of life's learning curves. Being a teen without the right understanding and love has a huge effect on the development of the brain and how we relate to everything and everyone later in life. We see everything as a threat; our brains process a million "what ifs" a second, and almost all of those ruminations are negative, which can be really draining on our souls. But I was made this way - this happened to me, and I had no control over how I turned out.

I often dream and think there is a different version of me that doesn't wake up at 5 a.m., startled by the slightest sound or movement in my house, and jump up, sometimes shouting out, ready for war. Or a version that just wakes up naturally without having a thousand thoughts flood instantly into my brain of every interaction or conversation I've had in the last week, analysing every word for ages, looking for hidden negative meanings or attitudes. A counsellor I see once said to my partner Pauline, "You must be exhausted," as I repeat things multiple times so my brain can process the threat level in absolutely everything. For example, when going to the cinema, my brain processes at lightning speed - how many people are there, who is sitting next to me, what if someone pulls out a knife and attacks us, what things could I use as a weapon to defend my family, where are the exits if there is a fire? Now, bear in mind this all happens in seconds. After fifty-some years, my brain has gotten good at it, but it's so draining, constantly being on guard for situations you know will never happen. But that's the hardware in your head - that's the computer you have been given. That's all my brain knows, and I will be like that for the rest of my life. It's why I love being alone. I go out most days after work or to cycle - I do twenty-five miles most days, as it allows my brain to calm a bit. But even then, circling thoughts seem to fill my head. But at least I'm free and on my own - I can focus on trying to calm my thoughts down. I have grown to love solitude, as I said before, but I would learn later in life that this is a part of C-PTSD. It's a way to cope and regulate the threats, whether real or imaginary, as your brain doesn't really know the difference. Either way, it's a stress response and anxiety overload that somehow takes you back to your youth and abuse - it's all that I know. Although it's messed up, there is comfort in that. I can't explain it; like I said, it's the way my brain works, and that is never going to change, no matter how much talking or therapy I do. But it does become more manageable, and at least now I recognise when I'm doing it and am aware it's C-PTSD making me think this. For most of my life, I had CPTSD and never knew it, and it's insidious how it controls you while you're unaware.

I had been going up to Thurso as my sister Kathleen had her own flat by then and kindly let me stay there some weekends when I wasn't at my pals', which allowed me to have a base where I loved being - my hometown, Thurso.

Around the age of fifteen, I was called into the office at the children's centre. I thought, "What have I done now?" and saw that two members of staff were sitting there, so I assumed it must be serious. They then asked how I felt about being fostered or placed in a family environment. By then, they thought I should be placed with someone because, in those days, when you turned sixteen, it was time to leave care and venture out into the real world to fend for yourself - that's where their responsibility ended.

I asked, "What do you mean?" and they told me they wanted me to write an advert in the paper asking for a family to take me in. As you can imagine, I wasn't happy with the idea of writing an advert begging for a family to look after me, but after a lot of persuasion, I reluctantly agreed. The advert was written up and put in the local paper, which, when I look back on it, I think was so wrong. Everyone saw it - all my friends and peers saw it - which was incredibly embarrassing for me, as I was very private about my life and past situation. Loads of people asked me about it and that left me feeling exposed and humiliated. But I guess the children's centre thought it was the best for me.

Anyway, a couple from Thurso wanted to take me in. They were an older couple, but they lived in Thurso, so it was arranged that I would stay with them for a couple of weekends to try it out. The lady was incredibly kind to me, but there was a massive generational gap. I was fifteen, loaded with all the baggage from the past, and had a deep mistrust of any kind of carer figure I wasn't sure about. But off I went, staying at their house at the weekends, which was good for me as I was home with my friends who, by then, were like family to me.

When it came to my birthday, they bought me a state-of-the-art record player stereo for my room, a load of the best tracksuits, and gave me £300 in cash for my bank account. It was unbelievably kind, but remember, I wasn't used to getting anything like that. I've never taken anything from anyone in my life, and often when I get a gift, I tend to give it away. So I found this really hard. I felt unworthy of kindness or any kind of affection or love, even though it was an act of kindness. My brain would not allow this, so I spiralled. Now, looking back, I know this was my C-PTSD at work, though at the time, I had no clue. I started to really struggle with feelings of not deserving anything, of not being worthy of kindness or gifts. Deep down, I would self-loathe, and my brain would constantly remind me that I didn't deserve any of this, just as Mrs Nobody had often reminded me that I was beyond worthless, that everyone hated me, that I was unlovable. So, I started to rebel - staying out every weekend, getting drunk with my pals, going to parties, and just being a teenager.

Not long after this, I had my first massive panic attack . I still remember it vividly, as it's burnt into my brain, like one of those "you know where you were" moments when something major happens. Me and the lady were coming home in her car, and my eye started twitching uncontrollably, which I now know is called fasciculation. But at the time, being fifteen, I thought I was going to die -

that this was some deadly disease that was going to kill me. Now, looking back, I realise the first actual panic attack I ever had was during a particularly brutal beating that me and my brother received from Mrs Nobody when my brother had accidentally thrown Rusty's bone through the window of the children's home, and it landed on the dinner table. But at the time, I was only about seven, and I didn't know anything about life, let alone what a panic attack was. But now, as I was in the car with her driving home, I recognised it for what it was - my heart started racing, my mouth went dry, I had that dropping feeling in my stomach, and I went white and started sweating. I never said anything her as I was gripped by pure, terrifying, blind panic, the kind where you can't even speak. We got home, and I went to my room, where I was awake all night, panicking as if someone had a gun to my head or I was about to fall off a high cliff.

I didn't know the people who took me in well enough at that point to trust them with what was going on with me, so I stayed quiet and totally withdrew from all normal activities. For the next two weeks, I stopped eating - only taking a bite or two from any meal made for me - so I lost a fair bit of weight. I was really thin at the time anyway, as all the breakdancing meant I had super low body fat. I just sat on their couch day and night until the lady got so worried about me that she made an appointment with my local doctor. I went to see my GP, and I told him what was happening. He explained that I was having a panic attack and that there was nothing wrong with me. After he reassured me that I was healthy and had no disease, I left the room, only to go back in after five steps, convinced I was going to drop dead before I got home. I was a mess, and no amount of talking could change the thoughts flying through my brain.

So, the GP prescribed antidepressants for me. When I got home, I showed them to Christine, and she took them and flushed them down the toilet, saying, "You don't want to go down that path." Panic attacks would stay with me for most of my life until many years later, when I learned how to control them, but they cost me dearly.

I was trying to function as a normal teenager with all that entails, but on top of that, I had dissociation, C-PTSD, and anxiety panic attack disorder. Life was so challenging, trying to process what was going on with me, but I was a teenager - I had no clue. Over time, I just started to get on with it and learn to live with the attacks. So, at the weekends, I would go out with my Thurso pals, and we would go up to the American bit at John Kennedy Drive and drink and party with all our American pals. Like I said, Kerry's mum was never in at the weekend as she worked on the American bases, so there were always loads of us staying over at hers with her pals and mine. Those were crazy times, but they took my mind off what I was going through. I would end up staying over at night, and that was not what the couple who I was living with wanted. She wanted me to go gardening with her and stay in and watch TV at the weekends.

Now, she was a lovely lady, and I'm so grateful for the kindness she showed me, but it was never going to work out. I was already messed up and rebelling against life, plus there was the age generation gap. By then, I had left the children's centre and was staying with them full-time.

I had left school in Wick on a Friday, and by Monday, I was enrolled in a Youth Training Scheme (YTS) where they taught you woodworking and building skills with a view to getting a job. We, of course, referred to the YTS as the "Young, Thick, and Stupid" scheme. I left school with two O-grades, in Art and English, as by my last year, I had bunked off more than I had attended. I found school and authority really hard to deal with. Like I said, I had been belted by so many teachers I lost count, and I was now immune to it - to the point where I would burst out laughing when I got belted. But at the same time, this was me becoming immune to physical hardship or pain. I had taught myself to be solid, and that's something that stayed with me the rest of my life. I have a high tolerance for physical pain, and that was me creating an iron shield against life's past beatings.

CHAPTER 7:

YOUNG, THICK, STUPID, YTS

The YTS was a blast - most of my pals were there, including my breakdancing mates. The YTS had two groups: the building side and the engineering group up in the huts on Wick Airfield. We were all good pals and would get moved about from time to time, but it was a madhouse with all the boys together. The laughs were brilliant. Me, Willie Millar, Donnie Murray, Gordie Green, Ronald Grey - all the boys were there, and the Thurso lads used to get the bus through in the morning from outside the job centre. The guy that taught us was called Mike, and he was from Yorkshire. He had a beard, smoked a pipe, and drove a big Range Rover. He was a top guy, and we all respected him, but boy, did he have his hands full with us.

We were learning everything from woodturning to welding to bricklaying. Looking back, I wish I had stuck in more because it was a great course, but every day was just a mad carry-on with the lads. Every Friday was payday, and the wages were £27.50 - what a joke, when I look back. A 35-hour working week for that! On a Friday, we would have an incinerator barrel in the backyard, and we would burn all the wood waste, etc. But we used to take a bike pump, suck up white spirits, and make homemade flamethrowers. Anything that wasn't nailed down went in the incinerator. One Friday, one of the boys found some normal-looking plastic sheets, stuck them in, and before we knew it, the fire brigade was there because the smoke was so thick you couldn't see the buildings. Just a normal day at the YTS.

The boys from the engineering and building sections were always pulling pranks on each other. One time, just before lunch, the worst smell ever was coming from our canteen room - someone had put a dead crow in our toasty maker and left it to cook. Like I said, that was normal. There are a hundred funny stories from that place, but good times, and life seemed a bit more stable.

On a Friday, we would head home, get a shower, then all go meet up at Willie Millar's house. Someone would go to the local shop to buy a bottle of vodka and some beers before we'd head out to see what madness we could get up to in Thurso. The strange thing is, there was always someone's house we could go to or a party, or we'd head up to John Kennedy Drive. There were plenty of girls around, and often the boys competed to see who would end up with the prettiest. Sometimes we would head out to Halkirk for the youth club discos, or spend weekends at Wick Youth Club. But there was never a shortage of things to do, with loads of laughs and endless backflips. Those were great times I look back on fondly.

I could do an off-the-wall back somersault as easily as scratching my head—by then, we had done thousands. It was the one thing guaranteed to impress people when we went out. It was a time in my life when I was really reckless, didn't care much about the future, and was just having as much fun as I could with my friends while trying to cope with panic attacks. I would drink most weekends, as did all my pals, but no matter how drunk we got, we never failed to practise our moves—we could still dance or do flips every time.

It got to the point where I wasn't coming back on weekends - I would go missing for a few days, and eventually, the couple who had taken me in had had enough and wanted me out of their house. I was never rude and was kind to almost everyone, but I had mentally checked out of the foster situation. By this time, I think I was beyond the point of fitting into a loving family home - it definitely wasn't for me. So, they contacted my social worker to have me removed. Looking back, it was a terrible idea from the start, but the powers that be thought placing me there was a good idea.

My social worker at the time came to get me, and the only place they could find for me was a small village called Papigoe, just under two miles from Wick, right on the coast. So, there I was, once again put away from all my Thurso pals, and now, even worse, it was in the middle of nowhere as far as I was concerned. At least I had my Wick pals, but to see them, as most lived on the far side of Wick, it was about a five-mile round trip. I would sometimes do that twice, even three times a day. I had to walk across the airfield runway to get to my job every morning at the YTS in Wick, no matter what the weather was like. Trust me, there were mornings with 90-mile-an-hour winds and hailstones belting me in the face - this is the far north of Scotland, after all, and right on the coast. One time when the snow was so deep that I couldn't tell where the road was - the snow was up to my thighs, and there was a blizzard. I didn't think I would find my way to work, it was that bad, but I had been warned about taking time off, so I had to go no matter what the weather.

Another day, I was walking along and saw a frozen pond in a field, so I decided to start doing windmills (a breakdance move where you spin on your shoulders with your legs going round super fast). A farmer passed by and stopped his tractor as I was breakdancing in the middle of his field, in the middle of nowhere. Looking back, I realise how bizarre it must have looked, but I used to practise all the time, no matter where I was.

Living out there was tough. I was on my own in a bed-and-breakfast type place, walking to a job where we barely got paid. After a year, I had had enough and thought, "I need to get a grip on life; this is not for me." My sister Ann had gotten back in touch at this point, and I told her life wasn't going in a good direction for me. She suggested I come to stay with her - she lived in East Anglia in England. I decided that anything had to be better than what I was doing, so I thought, as soon as I get my next YTS pay, I'm heading to England.

At the time, in the bed-and-breakfast place I was staying, there was a group of New Zealand guys who were travelling through Europe and were staying there for a few weeks, doing tree planting for money. It tied in with the time they were leaving to head to England, so I asked if I could get a lift with them, as my YTS wages wouldn't cover a train ticket or bus fare. One of the guys said, "Yeah, we're going to Manchester for a wedding, and there's space if you want to come along." So, the decision was made - I worked the week, packed what I could carry in a backpack, and off we went.

I had never been to England before, and I was only seventeen, but I thought, "What the heck, time to venture off in life. There's nothing to look forward to up north for me." So, we travelled down to England, and I called my sister and told her I'd be down to hers on Friday or Saturday. At that point, I just guessed how long it would take me.

When we got to Manchester, we stayed in a rough housing scheme that night with some girl I had never met, but the tree planters seemed to know her, so I stayed there the first night. I was deciding how I was going to get to this place called Halesworth, which I had never heard of. I had run out of money, as I had to use some for petrol and the rest for food. So, I jumped on a train towards East Anglia and made it as far as I could on the few pounds I had left. I got off at a random station, walked to the first houses I could see, and knocked on a random door to ask which way it was to Halesworth. They had never heard of it, so I said it was near Lowestoft, and they told me to follow a certain road, which I did. I was about forty miles away from Halesworth, so I thumbed a lift again, and a guy stopped. He turned out to be a priest or minister or something. As we got talking, I explained I had a sister called Ann who owned a wine shop in Halesworth, and I needed to get there. I think he felt sorry for me, and what was really kind of him was that he took me twenty miles out of his way to Halesworth and dropped me off at a group of houses as we entered the town.

I thanked him for his kindness and thought I'd knock on the first door I found, which I did. A lady answered, and I said I was looking for a lady called Ann who owned a wine shop. The lady said she wasn't sure, but there was a lady called Ann who lived a couple of streets up, and I could try her. So, I located the house, knocked on the door, and, luckily, it turned out to be the right house, which is amazing, as if I had been dropped off anywhere else, it would have been really hard to locate my sister's house. It was one of life's bizarre pieces of good luck.

It had taken the best part of two days to get to Ann's, but I was just relieved to be there. It was my first time in England and so far from my home county. When I arrived, my brother Andrew was already there with my sister Kathleen, who had arrived a few days before me. My sister lived there with her husband Alex at the time, and their two kids, Penny and Joanna. It was a proper family home - large, with a beautiful garden. Ann showed me to my room, which was next to my brother Andrew's room. She made me some food, and my new life in England was about to begin.

The first thing I needed to do was find work, so I spent a few days going around asking if anyone had any jobs available. Eventually, I was offered a job placement at the local carpet fitting shop in the centre of town. As much as I had plans, being a carpet fitter wasn't one of them, but needs must, and I wasn't afraid of hard work to get ahead in life. If I had thought Thurso was a quiet, small town, Halesworth was going to be a shock to my system. The population was about four and a half thousand, and it was really a sleepy English market town, but it was beautiful - just very different from my hometown of Thurso, the most northerly town in the UK. The people were different, the accent was completely different, and, as I would later find out, if you weren't from there, you were an outsider no matter how long you lived there. But for now, this was home, and I was determined to make the most of the opportunity my sister Ann had given me.

So, I took on the job at the carpet shop and turned up on Monday morning, unsure of what to expect. The boss, Dennis, introduced himself and said I was going to be learning from Garry. Surprisingly, Garry and I got along great, which was unusual for me as I normally take a long time to warm up to people. But he was a good laugh and was teaching me a new skill, so it was a positive start for me. I loved the change of life, and the climate was so much warmer than Thurso. The long, beautiful summers and milder winters were a welcome change from the harsh Highland climate.

The first thing Garry said to me was that we needed to load up the underlay for the first job. I said no worries, and we headed to a storage shed down a small dirt road at the back of the shop where we kept the rolls of underlay. We loaded up ten rolls of underlay into the long-backed van and lifted two rolls of carpet. Straight away, I thought, "I like the heavy lifting and manual graft." So off we went to the first job. Over the weeks and months, Garry taught me the basics of carpet fitting, and I got pretty good at it. What I loved about the job was that every day I was in a different house, which appealed to my need not to stay in one place too long - a common trait among those with C-PTSD.

At that time, I was really quiet and kept to myself. I didn't communicate much and was described by others as a bit of a loner. I would put on my Walkman and say as little as possible to people I didn't know well. But I enjoyed the job - it was hard graft but fun, and I got along well with Garry, who kind of looked out for me, which I appreciated. Life was looking up. Living with my sister was good; she really looked after me, making me a great breakfast in the morning and a packed lunch every day, which was really kind of her. That's the type of person she is - kind and caring. Life seemed more stable than it had been in a long time.

My original Kuk Sool membership card which I still have

CHAPTER 8:

KUK SOOL WON

At this time, I was looking to start martial arts, as I had been a huge fan of Bruce Lee. By this time, breakdancing had kind of died out, so my next adventure was to become the best at martial arts. Because of my rough start in life, I had a burning desire to make my mark, to be someone, and to prove wrong all the people who had told me I would achieve nothing in life. It's a strange thing, but I wanted to prove to myself most of all that I was worthy and good enough - that I wasn't that little scared boy alone in the pitch-black cupboard, terrified in the dark. I had decided to become untouchable, bulletproof, and to make others' criticisms of me irrelevant.

By now, I was already in incredible shape from years of breakdancing. I had about four or five percent body fat, a six-pack to die for, and could do amazing things with my body. Now, at fifty-four, I realise that at the time, I was really quiet and deep down lacked social confidence in life, though not in myself. Years later, I read in my care home report that they thought I was big-headed, but they couldn't have been further from the truth. I put on a bravado to cover my insecurities and self-doubt, but I was developing a "don't mess with me" attitude. I had spent thousands of hours in single-minded dedication, mastering all the breakdance moves and becoming one of the best. This was dedication at the highest level. I would practise anything I wanted to learn until I became good at it, often long after my friends had gone home. That fire burned deep in my soul - to prove to myself and the world that I was relevant and worthwhile. When I performed a move, it was like saying, "Wait till you check this out - I'm not like other people. I'll show you who I am through the expression of physicality."

Martial arts totally appealed to me. For years, I had watched the old kung fu movies where the weakling would get beaten up, then meet a mystical master, learn an incredible fighting style, and go back to defeat those who had wronged him. It was a metaphor for my life - I would never let anyone harm me in any way, physically or mentally, and if they tried, it would come at a huge cost to them.

So, I started going down to the local leisure centre in Halesworth most weekends for a pint with my brother after work on Friday and Saturday nights. While I was there, I noticed a photocopied poster with a picture of a guy throwing another guy, and the words "Kuk Sool Won" written on top. I thought, Kuk Sool Won? That's a weird name for a martial art. I'd heard of Kung Fu, Karate, Tae Kwon Do, etc, but never this. The combination of the picture and the esoteric name instantly attracted me because I've never been one to follow the pack - I've always wanted to do something different. The poster said classes were held there on a Saturday or whatever day it was, so I showed it to my brother and asked if he'd come with me. I kind of lacked the confidence to go alone for the first class. One, I didn't like meeting new people, and two, I hated talking to people I didn't know at the best of times. My brother said, "Yeah, no problem."

So, I nervously waited until the day of the class. The day before, my brother and I were at the leisure centre, and I put a pound in the fruit machine - boom! I won fifty pounds, which was more than my wages. I thought, Yes, nice one! I'll have money to spend on something this week.

The next day, I headed down to the hall where the martial arts class was going to take place. I saw a few people lined up outside in black martial arts uniforms with patches on the back that said "Kuk Sool Won" in an arch shape over the shoulder, with a fist emblem in the centre. I thought, Wow, this looks cool. These guys look the business. I went in and saw a guy in the corner with a line of people going up to him, bowing, and paying for their lessons. This guy looked like he could beat anyone up - super focused and intense, but also welcoming in a disciplined kind of way. When it was my turn, he said, "Hello, I'm Martin Ducker. I'm the instructor here. Are you here to try the class?" I said, "Yeah, this is my brother's and my first time." He said, "Come back next week," which was a bit disappointing, but we left and came back the following week, eager to start lessons.

Master Martin said, "Line up at the start of class; we will begin shortly." The class started with bows and Korean commands to the flags at the front, so my brother and I just followed along. I had never been somewhere so intense and focused. It was very regimented and strict but also ordered and purposeful. From that first bow, I was totally hooked. This was what I had been searching for my whole life. I just knew I had never felt more at home in my life than in that training hall that night.

We proceeded with the bows, then did the warm-up and stretching. I was already pretty flexible from all the years of breakdancing and was in amazing shape overall, so I thrived. We went through kicking routines, punching drills, acrobatics - I was loving it. Halfway through the class, we were to face our partner and gently tap them with a kick to the leg or a light tap to the face. But my brother and I were belting the heck out of each other until the instructor came over and said, "You guys need to calm down a bit." My brother and I just looked at each other and smiled.

We got through a really sweaty class, and I went over to the instructor, now known as Master Martin Ducker, but at the time, he was a first-degree black belt or "Jyo Kyo Nim." I'll refer to him as Master Martin for ease of writing. He asked if I enjoyed the class, and I said I loved it and asked how I could join. Luckily, I had the fifty pounds I'd won from the fruit machine the week before, so I paid for my membership, suit, and badges straight away. I knew this was my calling.

That night, I went out into my sister's garden and showed her all the moves I had been learning, practising late into the night - probably until two in the morning -

since everyone had gone to bed. Luckily, my room had a small door that led right out into the garden without having to go through the house, which was awesome.

I started attending regularly, never missing a class and training until I was a puddle of sweat every session. Classes back then were a lot different than they are now - really hard physical training, with no showing of weakness, and super strict discipline. Like I said, I was thriving, and it wasn't uncommon at the end of class for moisture to be running down the walls from all the sweat. What I loved was that Master Martin had a way of bringing out the best in people. He made you push to your limits and encouraged you to go past your comfort zone to achieve the next level.

I loved the "firsts." I remember Master Martin saying to me, "Do a no-handed cartwheel." No one in class could really do it, and I had never done one before, although I could do as many backflips in a row as I wanted or front somersaults over the back of someone. Anyway, on the first attempt, I fell. But I got up and practised the rest of the class, doing the same flip. At the end, Master Martin got me up in front of the whole class and said, "Do it," and I flipped and landed on my feet. Everyone applauded, and I had that great feeling of respect. There were many moments like that in every class, whether it was a hard sparring session - and sparring was a lot rougher back then - or learning a new kick, form, or technique.

Master Martin was all about drilling you repeatedly until it was perfect, and that served me well in life. Now I specialise in joint locks and am known for them, but I learned from my instructor to never use strength, but instead to use technique, and drill your martial arts until they're perfect. At the time, Master Martin taught classes with his wife, Alison Ducker. She played a massive part in guiding not only my martial arts but also me as a human being and how I related to other people. She was a unique balance of warrior on the mats and life coach off the mats. I've never met anyone like her since and feel blessed to have had her and Master Martin as my guides throughout my life and martial arts journey. I owe them so much and am eternally grateful for their guidance. Master Martin is the closest thing I've had to a father in my life and has been there for me unconditionally, as has Master Ally, through good times and bad.

I never talked much about my past to anyone, including my instructors. But later in life, when I was in my fifties and going through some tough times, Master Martin said to me that he knew there was something hidden, something there. But I wouldn't tell him until nearly forty years after our first meeting. I was that closed off and private about my past.

Things were fairly stable for me, and martial arts helped me keep some of the CPTSD symptoms at bay, but they were never far away. One night, I decided to go uptown for a game of pool and to chill at the leisure centre. When I arrived, there was a group of about ten local kids around my age. I put my money on the pool table to wait for my turn. After waiting for a while, when it was about my turn, one of the guys put his money in before mine, even though I was next. I said, "I'm next, mate," and the guy instantly gave me some bullshit remark. I repeated that it was my turn, and one of his pals said, "Fuck off, you Scottish prick."

So instantly, it was on. I said, "Make me," and the guy came over, but before he could do anything, I cracked him in the jaw, dropping him like a sack of potatoes. Then, all of them started laying into me. By now, the person behind the bar came over, kicked me out, and they followed me, shouting stuff about me being Scottish and how they were going to beat the crap out of me. They were yelling, "You better piss off back home," etc. I wasn't bothered; I'd been in this situation so many times that it didn't faze me in the slightest. So, I went back home and told my brother Andrew, and he was like, "Let's go." He picked up a suitable weapon that was lying in his room - I think it was a dumbbell bar - and off we went.

When we got there, he went in and said, "Who was starting on my brother?" A few of them came outside, and Andrew was like, "Come on then." Not one of them stepped forward. The tense standoff lasted a few minutes, with both me and Andrew ready for a war, which by now we were well used to and even looked forward to. But they all went back inside once they realised Andrew was serious. One thing I know about my brother and me is that we don't fear anyone. If you want to try and intimidate or hurt us, you're going to have a really, really bad day. The only thing that bothered me was if Master Martin found out, but luckily, someone else had seen what happened earlier and told the bar staff that they had started on me, so they were happy to forget what happened.

Actually, the guy I had punched came up to me a few weeks later and apologised, admitting he had been out of order. That was that resolved, and on the scale of things, there was never any trouble after that in Halesworth. Like I said, I was a closed book and kept myself to myself, but I was hypervigilant to the possibility of any kind of threat, real or imaginary. I would use the memory of any insult, intimidation attempt, or anything trying to put me down as fuel in training. It would push me and motivate me to ignore tiredness, pain, or any kind of weakness on my part. I would eliminate any and all weaknesses I could physically, but the brain keeps a score of the past. No matter how much you think you can block it out, you can't. There is a price to be paid for ignoring trauma, and I would learn in life that your body will make you face up to the past one way or another.

One night my brother and one of his work pals took me out to Lowestoft, a seaside town that was busy at the weekends. Just before we went into the nightclub, I had a massive panic attack, completely out of the blue - no warning, nothing. My breath just disappeared. I went white and sweaty, losing the power in my legs like I was going to fall over, and the worst part was that I was miles away from home. So I said to my brother, "I need to go," but I had to wait for a lift back as it was about nineteen miles away. I went to the seafront and sat on a bench as I didn't want to ruin my brother's and his friend's night. I sat in blind, terrified panic for about three hours before they came back. I never said anything. This was on a Friday night, and we headed back to Halesworth. When we got home, I just went to bed, staying up the whole night - heart racing, feeling sick, in a mad panic without knowing what I was panicking about.

In the morning, because I had been up all night with adrenaline running through me, I had really bad guts. It was about time for Kuk Sool class, and my brother knew I would never miss training, so he came to find me on the toilet, being sick and ill, and asked me what was wrong. I told him, and he tried his best to reassure me, but he knew how bad it was and said I needed to make an appointment with my doctor straight away, which I did. It was my first time seeing a doctor in Halesworth, so I had to register, and I got a doctor I'll call Doc M.

When I went in, he asked me what was wrong, and I blurted out what had been happening. He said, "I see from your notes that you suffer from anxiety and panic attacks," and I explained how bad they had been in Thurso. He was so kind and understanding. He said, "Come back at six when we close, and I can help you." So, I came back, and he did a self-hypnosis relaxation thing with me, which brought me a bit of comfort. Every week after that, we did the same thing, teaching me to do deep breathing while willing my muscles to let go of the tension and stress. Over time, this helped immensely, and I could kind of recognise and semi-control the severity of the panic attacks. He was so kind to take his own time to help me. I think he could see the anxiety in me. He asked me about my past, and I told him my parents had died when I was a baby. (I would later find out my real dad hadn't died, but I'll go into that later. For now, I thought he was dead.) He asked me to talk about it, and I stopped going back to the sessions. I thanked him for the help and said I was fine, but really, I didn't want to have to talk about the past. It was buried, and that was where it was going to stay, but he helped me so much.

My inspirations Master Martin & Master Alison Ducker

Me and Master Martin after 40 years of training

On a visit to my Falkirk school a few years back

An eager young student in halesworth

CHAPTER 9:

HOMESICK

Funny how when you look back at some of your toughest times, life is punctuated with good people who help you on your journey, and also those who don't. But it's all part of life's rich tapestry and gives us perspective on life, its meaning, and our place in it. Panic attacks or anxiety disorders are actually mental health conditions, and it's hard for people to speak about them, especially young guys brought up in the Highlands where, years ago, things like that were not talked about. I wish I could go back to then and let myself know that it was going to be okay, as living in panic and heightened anxiety is a cruel thing for a teenager to have to endure. There is a cost to the things that happen to people who suffer any type of abuse from a young age. I've seen what it's done to the people I grew up with. The cost of untreated mental health conditions can cost people their lives, and a few of the people I grew up with decided they couldn't carry on in life and that it was too painful. This makes me really sad - they were let down by the people who were meant to care for them in their time of need, but no one was there for them; they were let down again.

I know when I opened up and sought help in life, I had to wait over a year to see a counsellor, and the wait for a mental health appointment to help with my CPTSD was at least two years. I find it breathtaking because the government employed the people who abused us, causing all the trauma in our lives, and then they say you have to wait years for any kind of help with that trauma. We wouldn't have it if it weren't for the carers who decided that beating on kids with terrible family situations was a good idea.

Life was fairly stable in Halesworth, and training was going great. Life at my sister's was good - lots of laughs and a fairly stress-free environment. One day, I was walking along the road to go to lunch, and Master Martin pulled up beside me in a car and asked if I wanted to help at a demo that day. I instantly said yes and went down to ask my boss if I could have the day off, which he agreed to. So off I went. I think it was for the rail company or something, but I remember being amazed and inspired watching some of the moves I hadn't seen before. My instructor was an exceptional martial artist, and I aspired to be like him. He was a great role model and gave me great guidance in life matters, even though I was super shut off from people.

I was training every moment I could, attending every single class, eating, sleeping, and breathing martial arts. At this time, my instructor told me the grandmaster and masters from America were coming over to do a seminar and asked if I would like to attend, to which I said yes. My head was filled with wonderment - what were they going to show at the seminar? What would I learn? I was so super excited.

The day arrived, so I jumped on the train and headed to Beccles, where the seminar was. When I got to the hall, I was really nervous because I didn't know at the time that anxiety disorders and CPTSD make you super wary of people, and I had actively tried to avoid big crowds in the last couple of years. But I overcame the fear with the excitement of the unknown, and when I went in, there were so many people from other schools. I hadn't realised it was so popular. Two of the martial arts instructors there were Master Jay Lee, a policeman from Houston, Texas, but also formidable in martial arts, and Master Marlin Simms, who was from Alabama, I think. He was awesome - very strict and loved really hard physical training, pushing people to their limits and then some.

We did the seminar, and Master Jay Lee was talking about spin force in techniques and mentioned it was like a breakdancer spinning on his back, which I thought was cool. I had never seen martial arts at such a high level. The night was finished with a demonstration, and I was blown away. After, we all got our certificates, which I still have - 1988. I left to get the train home, doing jumping kicks at everything above head height on the way home. I was floating on cloud nine, dreaming about getting my black belt. I was only a white belt beginner, just getting ready to promote to yellow belt - it took much longer back then to get to your first full belt. But I knew one day I'd be a black belt - that much I knew for sure. And I was the only Scottish person practising back then, so it fitted in perfectly for me, doing something different.

I have fond memories of my time in Halesworth, in part due to the stable home life I had and in part because my brain was occupied with work and training all the time. I tried to keep myself super busy. After a year or so, I started missing my Thurso friends and my hometown, so I decided it was time to leave Halesworth. Looking back, life was good there, but people with CPTSD have a habit of destroying good things or moving on when things are going well. It's a lot to do with feeling unworthy of happiness - I learned that years later from my psychologist, but at the time, I had no understanding of mental health or anything like that.

I spoke with my sister and explained my feelings, and she said she would be sad to see me go. I also spoke with my instructors, Master Martin and Master Ally. Master Martin said he would be sad to see me go and even offered me a place to stay at his house if I needed it. But I explained that I was homesick, and by then, I had that restless feeling I've had all my life - the urge to move away and start fresh. Remember, this was long before mobile phones or the internet - better times, I think. People had to phone you directly, and if you didn't have a phone, then there was no communication, which suited me back then.

I decided to move back, as my sister Kath had a flat in Thurso, so I moved in with her, which was good as it gave me a place to stay. Not long after, my sister moved away, and I was staying in the flat with one of my brother's pals, Stuart. We weren't supposed to be staying there, as my sister had handed in the keys, but we stayed for a few months anyway. I had no money and no job, so I was skint and couldn't even afford to eat. There were days when I wouldn't eat at all, and I would get food where I could. My pals would bring over things from time to time, as I didn't have a penny and hadn't signed on the dole or unemployment benefit.

I didn't tell people I wasn't eating much, as I didn't want anyone to feel they needed to help me, so I just said nothing. But when it got too bad - like if I hadn't eaten for a couple of days - I would visit people, and they would make tea and biscuits. Once whilst at Donnie's granny's house, and I was so hungry that I asked him for something to eat. In the fridge, there was a block of cheese and some onions, so I ate a bit of cheese with onion, and it tasted amazing because I was so hungry. I still eat that to this day - it's strange. Now, I could have asked my sister, but again, I didn't want to be a burden on anyone. She would have helped me, but I've never asked for help like that from anyone, not even family.

After a while, the housing association came around to evict us. By that time, I was eighteen and had just gotten a job at the local freezer factory called Norfrost. It was hard physical work making chest freezers, and you had to be fast to keep up with the production line. But the good thing was that at 10 am, you would get a tea break and could choose between a sausage roll or a pie to eat with it. A few girls I worked with on the tank line, which made the insides of the chest freezers, would give me their pies or sausage rolls, which was great as it meant regular food. We also got lunch every day, which was great because, in my first week of work, I didn't have a penny. The bus in the morning was a free company bus.

The issue was that I didn't have an alarm clock, so I had to try to wake up naturally before the 7 am pick-up. I asked a neighbour to knock on the door before they went to work, which worked out well. My first pay packet was about £120 - not much for the super hard graft in a factory, but when you're skint, it felt like a fortune. So, on my first pay packet, I went out and bought sausage, chips, and beans from the Central Restaurant in Thurso. Then I bought an alarm clock from Thurso's version of Poundland. It was one of those with two bells on top and a hammer in between, sounding like World War III when it went off, but it did the job.

By this point, breakdancing had died out, and there was only karate in Thurso, which wasn't for me, so I practised on my own. At the time, I had a new circle of friends. One of my pals was James Lynch, or Lynchy, who worked at Norfrost. I had known him since he moved from Glasgow to Thurso. I'd actually known him since I was about twelve or thirteen, and we hung out from time to time, but he was more into punk and stuff, while I was with my breakdance pals. We had always been friends, so we started hanging out. There was also another guy called Stevie Reid, who lived in Thurso East. I think he was pals with or related to my old school pal Tommy Reid - yeah, the one I had persuaded to piss in the school sandpit.

Stevie lived about a mile from Thurso, and he and Tommy were doing karate together at the time. But we started hanging out and became the best of friends - inseparable. We would go over and stay at Stevie's house most weekends. His mum, Joan, and dad, Big Dougie, were great with us - feeding us and looking after us when we were over at his house. Actually, at Christmas, Joan would invite me over to stay and even bought me a Christmas present - a truly lovely family. Stevie's brother was also called Dougie, but we called him Shougs - a great guy.

At the time, Tommy was hanging out with us a lot at the weekends as well, and we had a kind of gang. Since we all did martial arts, we were called "the Wongs" by the locals. Not politically correct now, but that's what we were known as. During this time, I had moved into a bedsit - one bedroom in a really old, run-down building. It was so cold in winter that the carpet, which was kind of damp, would freeze because I had a broken window that let the cold air come right in. There were times I thought I'd be found frozen to death, as that place was almost as cold as sleeping outside. But my pals and I would meet up on a Friday, ready for the weekend there.

Normally, James and I would jump off the bus from work and head around to where Stevie worked at a local garage. Then we would head up to the local Chinese restaurant for food and a pint before going to get ready and all meeting back at my bedsit to blast tunes and drink before heading out into town for madness, which usually involved drinking, fighting, and girls.

We lived as though each weekend was our last, all of us irresponsible and out to have the best time possible. Thurso, despite being a small town, could be a rough place at times - full of the best people, but not ones to take any nonsense. At the time, we were involved in so many fights that I couldn't recall them all. We never went out looking for trouble or started fights, but if anyone messed with us, it was on. We would head to the local nightclub at the end of the night, then either crash at Stevie's or, as a last resort, mine.

During this time, I was far from my instructor, who was based at the other end of England. So, I got in touch with a Kung Fu instructor who had moved up west, and I asked him about starting classes in Thurso. He eventually agreed, and so me and the boys began training in Thurso Town Hall a couple of nights a week. The instructor was good, but he had some strange training methods, which usually involved a lot of pain. For example, he would kick you hard between the legs while you stood in a horse stance, just to see if you could take it. Or he would slap your bare back as hard as he could or kick you in the stomach to see if you could handle being winded. Looking back, I realise it was all pointless, but at the time, I thought this was the path to becoming unbeatable and solid.

There weren't many people training with us, partly due to how demanding the training was, but a local lad named Gavin Chung, whose dad owned the local restaurant, came along. He later started training with me in Kuk Sool. My life consisted of long, hard shifts at the freezer factory, followed by my own training sessions, which would last three to four hours every day, plus martial arts classes a couple of times a week.

One time, the instructor asked me to lie on the ground with my legs slightly off the ground, and he jumped on my stomach from a height. I had a really strong midsection but was badly winded, though I tried not to show it. At that moment, my mind flashed back to all the beatings I had taken from Mrs Nobody, and any respect I had for him went out the window. After a while, we stopped training with him and looked for something else. We eventually found a Kung Fu instructor from Orkney who was really good - he practised Hung Kuen Kung Fu. So, me and the boys decided to go over to Orkney to start training with him. We were offered a place to stay with one of his students, Marty, and another guy called John.

After work, we got the Ola, the ferry from Scrabster to Orkney. There were massive waves that day, and it felt like you were flying when you jumped on the boat. We arrived at the place where we were staying, and it was cool because Marty had a training hall in his house, which was fairly big. That night, we all headed out into Kirkwall to sample the nightlife and hit the local nightclub with our new friends. The next day, we had a really tough training session for four or five hours, but when you're eighteen, you can go out all night and still train hard the next day. Our instructor worked us really hard, but that's the way we liked it. Over the next few weeks, we continued heading over to Orkney, training and partying in equal measure.

Around this time, one of the pubs in Thurso ran a talent competition on Sunday nights, and I had been entering by breakdancing, which I won every week. First prize was a large bottle of vodka, which I just stashed under my bed -

by the time the next trip came about, I had about six of them under there, much to the surprise of my pals.

Me and Frank sparring

Bag work coached by Frank

Me and Stevie Reid, my face burst after another fight

Me and James Lynch (or Lynchie) as he is known in The Wongs

CHAPTER 10:
DON'T F*** WITH THE WONGS!

One particular weekend, we headed out to the Orkney nightclub - me, James, and Stevie. We were sitting in the club, chatting with a group of local girls. I was on a seat near the table, Lynchy was opposite me, and Stevie was sitting to the left of me, talking to a girl. Suddenly, I noticed a group of guys standing next to me, but I didn't pay much attention. The next second, I saw something flying over the top of me. I quickly turned around to see that Stevie had jumped off his seat over my head and landed a flying headbutt on this big guy standing right next to me, instantly breaking his nose. It was bent at an unusual angle, with blood pouring out of it.

The guy, who was built like a tank, threw a punch towards me, which I blocked with my forearms. Then I got up and started palm-heeling him in the face. By now, James was up, and we were in a pitched battle with a load of guys we later found out were in the army. They had wanted to chat with the girls we were sitting with and had said something to Stevie earlier while he was at the bar, but he hadn't mentioned it to us as it seemed irrelevant. The bouncers jumped in, and it turned into a war. Eventually, we all got kicked out, and a massive fight broke out on the street - people fighting everywhere. The police came in force and dispersed everyone.

We were staying with John in a wee village outside of town and had to catch a bus. So, we all got on and grabbed a seat. I had a cream long-sleeved top on that was splattered with the guy's blood from the fight. We sat down, and then, lo and behold, the guys we had been fighting with got on the bus and sat directly behind my seat. I said to James, "Be ready, this is going to kick off." Every so often, one of the guys would grab the headrest as if he was about to get up, but they never said anything directly. The guy whose nose was broken wasn't there, but we knew these were his mates. I was sitting, ready for a punch or a grab - Lynchy and Stevie were ready too - and we waited for the inevitable. After a while, we got to our destination, jumped up, and hurried off the bus. Those guys probably thought we had chickened out, but as soon as we got off, we stood there and waited. The guys just walked right past us, saying nothing, so we just left it. Another wild night for the Wongs, but pretty standard at that time. We lived life hard but were brothers who would defend each other to the end, and that was just the kind of guys I needed in my life. I felt like I belonged.

Again, I never discussed my past, not even with those closest to me. I had buried it so deep in the back of my mind that although it was always there, I wouldn't dwell on it too much. Later in life, a friend who had gone through some traumatic things told me that he used to fight a lot, which is common in people with PTSD. It's a defence mechanism that's gone wrong - you're hard-wired to perceive threats, and you analyse every word or situation looking for hidden dangers. His psychologist asked him if he self-abused, to which he replied, "No."

The psychologist then said, "What do you think all the fights are about, then?"

I was told a similar thing years later. People with CPTSD often develop an attitude that if anyone tries to intimidate or hurt them, they go into war mode and will take on anyone or anything. When they were young and defenceless, they couldn't fight back, but later in life, they can, and in my case, that was extreme. I took no nonsense from anyone and was unafraid of anyone. In fact, it was in those combat situations where I felt calm, in control, and sure of myself. As weird as that may seem, that's the way it was.

I had applied to the council for better accommodation, as the place I stayed in was a dump - damp and freezing in winter, with no running water a lot of the time, so life was pretty tough. I used to go to the local hotel every night and get sausage, chips, and beans. Along with the food I got at the freezer factory, at least eating wasn't an issue like before. I eventually got a studio flat in Moorside Avenue, which was a nice place, and I moved out of the bedsit. Life was pretty good there - working and training, and at weekends, partying with the boys. At the time, there were lots of girls around. I had never really been in a serious relationship; I was too guarded, and after a few weeks, I would move on to the next. This, too, was part of the

CPTSD - it's common not to form attachments, but at the time, I didn't know this.

I met a girl who was a bit older than me - I was eighteen, and she was twenty-nine. She had two kids, and we started meeting up and chatting, gradually getting closer. One night, she ended up at mine during a party, and we kind of started seeing each other. After a few weeks, she asked me to move in with her, which I did. Looking back, it was a dumb thing to do, but I was young and drifting, so I moved in, and we started living together. At that time, I was also working at the local freezer factory, Norfrost, and training at night - running and working on pads, etc.

During this period, I got back in touch with Master Martin and explained that I was missing Kuk Sool and training with him. I mentioned that we had a group of about twelve students who used to meet up and train together, and I asked if he would be willing to open a Kuk Sool school in Thurso. Bearing in mind it was a 664-mile journey - a nearly twelve-hour drive - he initially said no. But after a couple of weeks, he changed his mind and said he would travel up to see me for some training. I was over the moon and eagerly awaited his arrival.

The day finally came, and Master Martin was to stay at my house. After getting off the train, he said he couldn't believe how far away it was or how cold it was. But we had a brilliant week of training and spending time together again. Of the twelve or so students, all were super dedicated and hard-working, which I think made a lasting impression on Master Martin. He seemed to really enjoy his trip, and hence, Kuk Sool Scotland was born way up in

Thurso. Master Martin would travel to Thurso many times, often bringing his family with him, and we would train hard wherever and whenever we could.

One time in February, it was freezing cold, and the hall was shut. Master Martin said, "We'll train on the beach."

Bearing in mind there was snow on the ground and it was freezing, we all went to the shore. Before we knew it, we were knee-deep in the ocean and doing throws into the water. We all loved it, but our feet were so cold when we came out that we couldn't even walk on the sand. Looking back, these are some of the best memories I have. Training was hard, but Master Martin seemed to bring out the best in me, giving me the focus and clarity I had been searching for all my life. In Kuk Sool, I was someone - no one could bully me or put me down. I trained so hard that I made my body a sheet of armour against anything life could throw at me, and mentally, Kuk Sool pushed me to become more than the sum of my parts through long hours of meditation and physical conditioning.

Ali Simpson, whom I had known from the breakdancing years, had joined, and we were always together, pushing each other to the limit to be the best we could possibly be. We had a great wee group, and the class started to grow and get stronger. We had a family join - the Smiths - and they all thrived in the training environment. Cathy Smith would eventually go on to become a master herself in Kuk Sool Won and still trains today, which is amazing.

Training was going great, but my personal life was a different matter. I think the age gap played a factor. I was with my girlfriend at the time for a year before that fell apart, and then I had to move out. I had given up my flat, so I was kind of stuck for a place to stay. I phoned up Christine, who had been so kind to me in the children's home, and I asked her if I could stay for a couple of weeks until I got back on my feet, which she kindly agreed to. She really was the best.

During this time, I was going out partying and having a wild time. I was young and didn't care about anything except training and having a good time, so life was pretty wild.

Walking along with Lynch one Saturday afternoon we accidentally stepped out in front of some guy's car. I waved and said, "Sorry, mate," but he wasn't having any of it and wanted to teach me a lesson. He got out of the car and started shouting, calling me everything under the sun. He was a big lump of a guy. Again, I said, "Sorry, it was an accident," but he kept shouting. I went over to shake his hand and apologise, but he threw a punch from behind his open door. I moved back instinctively - by now, I had really sharp reactions - and instantly threw a backfist to the side of his head without thinking. His head split wide open, and that was the end of that. I said to Lynch, "I gave him a chance," but Lynch was used to it by now; fighting was a way of life, and there was usually some madness happening. To us, it was normal.

By now, I was about a red belt in Kuk Sool, and my lifestyle was catching up with me. The final straw was when my brother Andrew and I were walking to the pub on a night out. Two guys drunk past us and started to talk shit. One of them called me something as we walked past them.

I turned and said, "What did you say?" and he repeated his drunken insult. So, I ran over and kicked him in the head with a high roundhouse kick, sending him flying back through a shop window. By now, the other guy had thrown a punch at my brother, and Andrew grabbed him and threw him through another window. A crowd had gathered, and Andrew had cut his arm pretty badly. I told him he needed to go to the hospital to get stitches, but my brother insisted we go get a beer like we'd planned. He eventually went to get a taxi, leaving a trail of blood drops everywhere.

Again, we didn't start the fight, but those guys chose the wrong two people to mess with. My brother and I had zero tolerance - absolutely zero - for anyone trying to put us down or start trouble with us. Well, by now, Master Martin had heard about all the fighting I was getting involved in, and the next time he saw me, he sat me down and said that if he heard of any more incidents, he was going to kick me out. I explained that I hadn't started the fights, but he said, "No more." This was going to be tough because I was hard-wired to respond to any threat with full-on retaliation. So, I stopped going out as much on weekends and avoided places where I knew trouble would start. I focused even more intently on training and only occasionally went out.

During this time, I met my second serious girlfriend. We met, and she asked me to give her a call, which I did. She told me she was married but in the process of leaving her husband before she met me, as she was unhappy, and I accepted that. We got on really well, so we started seeing each other, and within a month or so, we moved in together. I moved out of Christine's, where I had been staying, and started the next chapter of my life. The guy she had been married to obviously thought I was the cause of the breakup, but I wasn't - she was already leaving him. This would obviously lead to conflict, but I wasn't bothered. For now, it was okay, and we settled into normal life.

At this time, I had really upped my training to insane hours a day and was at my physical peak. Life was going pretty well - my girlfriend was working, and I was teaching Kuk Sool classes at night and training all day. We lived in the centre of Thurso, in a flat above a shop. There were two flats - ours, and the one opposite where two guys lived. We shared the same tiny hallway leading to the stairs that took you outside. At first, everything was cool, but the guys next door liked to party until four in the morning and blast their music loudly. I asked them multiple times to turn it down, which they did while I was at the door, only to turn it up again soon after I left. My girlfriend worked early, and it constantly woke us up. In my mind, it was pure disrespect, and there was only so long I was going to put up with that.

Before long, things kicked off. My girlfriend and I were coming home one night, and we found the two guys on the stairs with a bag of chips, some of which had been dropped on the steps. I told them to pick them up, but they replied with some smart-arse comment. So, I squared up to them, and one of them threw a punch, which missed. I started punching the side of his head. My girlfriend had just opened the door, and they pushed me into the hallway of my house. All the while, I was punching the first guy non-stop. He was a bit bigger than me - I think I was ten stone at the time, but it was pure muscle and tendon. We battled down the hall, and I fell into my bedroom at the bottom of the hall. I still had the guy by the hair, punching as hard as I could, and he was trying to get away. I was holding him in a headlock when the other guy started kicking me in the side of the head while I was on the ground fighting - basically cheap shots. After four or five kicks, I let the first guy go, and he ran past the other guy to get to their flat.

While the second guy was still kicking me in the head, I grabbed a set of wooden nunchuks that were sitting by my bedside and belted him over the head, opening it up like a can of baked beans. Blood splattered up the wall and even reached the ceiling. He ran off, and they locked themselves in their flat while I pounded on their door, looking to finish what they started. They never came out, and the next day, I had the CID (Criminal Investigation Department) at my door, as the guy had gone to the hospital. The CID took my statement and my partner's as well. When they came into my house, they said it was self-defence and could see that we were a normal couple, not troublemakers, so there were no charges. A few hours later, the guy came to my door with a big bandage wrapped around his head, and we settled the beef then and there. I would never leave any disrespect unanswered - this was ingrained in my soul. I would rather die than back down.

After that, things went quiet for a while, and we got on with normal life. Eventually, we were offered a flat down near the beach on Swanson Street, which we took and moved into. Back then in Thurso, trouble would seem to find you for various reasons. In my case, it was because I did martial arts, which put a target on my back for some locals. One night me and Ali Simpson were out in the central chilling after training when a guy had moved up from Newcastle and thought he was a hard man came up giving me shit that he heard I was a martial artist and he wanted to fight me I just ignored him but then he tried to kick me in the balls but I grabbed his foot and swept him to the ground hovering my fist away from his face telling him I was the wrong person to start crap with I had completely forgot about this event until Ali reminded me recently when I called him up telling him I was writing this book that's the strange thing it all blurs into one but like I said I never started the fights but I definitely would never give in if they were looking for a fight I gave it to them it could be as simple as someone not liking you and at the weekend when they fill of beer there bravery gets the better of them. If you went out on weekends, before too long, there would be some kind of incident.

Later in life, I realised that CPTSD made me the way I was - hardwired to go straight to war at the slightest insult or verbal threat. I was ready to bring it on and see how it worked out for the other guy. When I was much younger, I was really quiet and not much of a fighter. But now, at nineteen, after all the battles me and the Wongs had been in, I didn't care - fighting never scared me. I think I was desensitised to physical pain due to what happened when I was young, and all the hard physical training I was doing every day. Pain had become my best friend, and I was determined to be bullyproof.

During this time, I had joined a gym in Scapa House and would spend hours there every day. That's where I met a guy called Frank McShane, who would later become my boxing coach. Frank was a small guy, but one of the fittest humans I have ever met. His endurance and physical skills were amazing, and I learned so much from him about training ethics and boxing. Up until this point, I was primarily a kicker and just average with my hands, so I definitely wasn't a natural boxer. During our first spar with the sixteen-ounce gloves - Frank hit me with a body shot that almost killed me. I was so winded I couldn't get up for ten minutes, but I was determined to get better. From then on, we trained regularly. Our sessions were about as hard as you could possibly push a human body, consisting of weights, lots of skipping, pad work, sparring, and stretching. Every session took you to the brink and sometimes past it, but my fitness became incredible during this time. After the session was over, I would often go for a run or to the beach and continue training for many hours after. I got to the point where I was doing things in the hundreds and was ultra-ripped and shredded.

Many years later, after I hadn't seen Frank for over thirty years, he cycled through to Falkirk to have a coffee with me. He cycled a round trip of seventy miles - he hasn't changed, still an absolute machine. I often look back, and Frank and I have talked about the insane level of training we did. I have never trained as hard in my life as I did then, and I'm so grateful for his guidance and lessons, which I have never forgotten. Frank was such a soft-spoken guy, but also wise in his advice and a great role model for me.

I'm lucky to have met the people who have taught me, and I value their lessons as they have made me who I am today. I owe them a lot.

At the time, I would train during the day, teach classes at night, and then go down to the beach and train until three or four in the morning. This was my life - this kept the demons in my head at bay, although they were always there under the surface. A friend from Thurso, Jock, lived on the beachfront, and he told me years later that he and his dad would watch me in the early hours training on the beach in the rain, snow, wind, or gales - it didn't matter what the weather was, I was there every day. He told me his dad said to him, "That boy is going places." I, of course, was oblivious to anything other than perfecting my craft and sculpting my body to be as good as Bruce Lee's. He had been a huge inspiration to me growing up, and at this time, my body looked just like his. I'm not bragging; this is just the truth - I was beyond driven, and I never got tired. There was a fire burning deep in my soul, almost a controlled rage deep within me. It was my way of shutting out all the past, and at this time, I never thought about the past, although it was ever present. It controls all your thoughts and decisions without you being aware of it, like a taskmaster deep in your psyche. All I thought about was creating a better life and future, and for the first time, I felt somewhat in control of my future. Training was my life - it was all I could focus on. It gave me a mental focus and a sense of calmness that nothing else came close to.

I remember one Christmas, I took the big bag of salt that was for the Christmas dinner and went down to the beach to salt the ice on the large group of steps so I could train later on Christmas Day. Thurso Beach has a group of steps going up to Victoria Walk along the top of the cliffs. I used to train there every day - running up them or squat-walking. One summer, a student and I spent the whole summer trying to walk up to the top on our hands in a handstand. It took us about five weeks, but we managed it. I liked challenges like that - whether it was doing an off-the-wall back somersault, a back sumi board break, or jumping over seven people bent at the waist and breaking a board. I was searching for that next impossible thing to do. I loved the challenge and the feeling of accomplishment after I achieved it, and then I would go straight on to the next impossible challenge. It was all about overcoming what others said was too hard or impossible to do - I loved the challenge.

At the time, most of my really good pals had gone off to join the army, and the only reason I hadn't was that I was teaching the only Kuk Sool Won class in Scotland at the time. This was around the time the Gulf War broke out, and they were shipped out to Iraq. One of my best pals, Stevie, would write to me all the time - this was before the internet - and he sent me a handful of sand from the Iraqi desert. It was a stressful time because I didn't know who would come back alive or not, and we were all a really tight group of pals. But when they got their first leave and came back, we would go out all weekend partying and having the best time ever before they had to head back to the uncertainties of war. Leaving was the worst part, and they would leave it to the last possible train so we could spend time together. Those were the best times - there would be twenty or so of us out in the Central Hotel in Thurso during the day, drinking and having a laugh as if they didn't have a care in the world. The best group of pals you could ever want, where fighting was never far away. But we were young and took zero shit from anyone. At the time, we were like family, and we looked out for one another - great times.

CHAPTER 11:

TO THE CAPITAL

Around this time, my instructor, Master Martin, announced that the British Championships for Kuk Sool were coming up. As this was the first time they were holding a championship, we decided to go down as a school to support and compete. I was eager to see how all the training had paid off, so for six months, I really pushed myself and my students. As the time drew closer, we decided to fundraise to help cover the cost of a bus to take everyone down to the championships. We all wore kilts, ready to show everyone how hard the Highlanders had been training.

It was a long coach ride to England, but we were motivated and fired up. We were going to stay in Master Martin's training hall, which meant we would get lots of training while we were there. I entered the tournament and competed in sparring, forms, techniques, and board breaking. I won three golds and one silver - not bad for my first tournament. It was a tough competition with huge sections, as loads of people entered since it was the first tournament. As a school, we dominated, with most of our students winning golds. I was hooked on the buzz of being someone and the recognition from my peers. All the hard work was worth it, and this marked the start of my competing years in Kuk Sool.

At the time, I realised that my education had suffered. Like I mentioned before, school and I did not see eye to eye, and I left with only a few O-Levels. I thought about doing something to improve my education, so a friend I trained with and I decided to enrol in a leisure and tourism course. I wanted to do something in health and fitness, but that was the closest thing they had to offer. So, it was back to a classroom environment for me. Every morning, I got up and went to study, trying my hardest to settle back into learning.

During the course, we learned everything from accounts to French to computing, which allowed me to gain other qualifications, including in English. On the whole, I did pretty well. That was literally our life we would study during the day and then martial arts training at night just training body and brain the moment we woke up to the moment we went to sleep. We even made a pact that no matter how tired or sore we were in the morning, as soon as we saw each other, we had to do a no-handed cartwheel. It was murder when we were aching from the day before, but that was the rule, and we stuck to it.

It was tough, as many memories resurfaced, and the same old demons haunted me, often triggering panic attacks. I did my best to manage these episodes through intense training and meditation. The course covered everything from accounting and French to computing, anatomy, and exercise science. It also enabled me to earn additional qualifications, such as Higher English and Computing, among others, and I did quite well overall. Reflecting now, I realise that my struggle in school wasn't due to a lack of intelligence; I was battling trauma, insecurity, panic attacks, and an overwhelming fear of everything. My brain was constantly catastrophising imaginary scenarios. Looking back, it breaks my heart to think of the pain I kept buried deep inside. I wish I could go back in time to reassure my younger self: "Don, it's okay. You've got this. You are enough, and you're doing your best with the hand you were dealt."

One memorable moment from the course was when a representative from a national sports organisation visited to test our fitness levels. My friend and I were in peak physical condition at the time, often performing hundreds of push-ups and sit-ups in our training routines, so we easily surpassed most of the existing high scores. The man was astonished by our performance and asked how we managed to reach such a level in such a remote place. At that time, my body fat was only four percent, and my resting heart rate was thirty-eight beats per minute. I was practically indefatigable, driven by an inner fire that seemed to fuel extraordinary physical feats. After a workout, I would often head to the beach to push myself further. When he asked, we simply replied, "All we do is train - all day, every day," and it was true. From morning until night, it was strange as training hard kept me balanced as the feelings of guilt shame and rage at past life horrors were never far away like a fire burning my soul and

I had to try to keep the rage internalised never letting anyone know what I was thinking or what was going on just under the surface

Our workouts were intense, and we set challenges for ourselves that seemed impossible. One of our favourites was to hang from Thurso footbridge over the river, competing to see who would drop first. We would hang on until our arms screamed for relief, faced with the choice of dropping into the river or pushing through the pain to pull ourselves back up. We constantly pushed our limits, training on the exercise bars at the river - doing four sets of fifty pull-ups - or performing dips that transitioned into handstand push-ups on the metal parallel bars, a feat we had seen gymnasts do on TV. Looking back, I am amazed at how driven I was, how determined to achieve the impossible. I realise now that much of my extreme physical conditioning was a way to cope with CPTSD and anxiety. At the time, I was entirely unaware of the trauma I had buried deep inside. I was intense, focused, and emotionally closed off, merely trying to survive from one day to the next. Yet I was driven to prove that I could overcome my brokenness through sheer hard work and pain.

Just as life in Thurso had begun to settle, my partner and I went to Jamaica for a three week holiday. It was my first time flying, and the thirteen-hour journey made me realise how much I hated being on a plane. Nevertheless, we arrived, and it was my first proper holiday abroad. The warm climate and good food were fantastic. Every evening, I would train, completing my self-imposed thousand-kick routine while the hotel security guards watched. One night, one of the guards who had been observing me approached in the resort's nightclub. He began boasting that he could beat me in a fight. I'd heard that sort of talk many times before from people looking for trouble, but I was wired never to back down from a challenge or threat, regardless of the consequences. At the back of the resort, there was an outdoor boxing ring. After listening to his provocations and boasting, I invited him to meet me there in the morning to prove his claim. He agreed, and a few of the tourists we had befriended expressed their interest in watching the match.

First thing in the morning, I headed up to the ring and waited for over an hour, but he was a no-show. Nevertheless, I was there, ready for whatever might come, no matter the cost. This stemmed from my determination never to let anyone threaten or intimidate me again. I didn't see him for the rest of the holiday, but I remained vigilant.

Another incident occurred at the resort, where cash wasn't used; instead, we paid with plastic shark tooth tokens. One morning, while I was out for a run, a local approached me, asking if I needed anything, like ganja or women. I laughed it off and declined, but he mentioned that he had some shark teeth tokens for sale at a cheaper rate. I thought it sounded good and agreed to meet him outside the resort. My girlfriend and I went to the arranged spot, paid for the bag of shark teeth, and noticed that the bottom felt soft. Opening it quickly, I discovered that it had been padded with cloth, with only a few tokens inside. I ran after the man and caught up with him, only to find that

117

three cars full of Jamaicans were now watching us. I realised the situation could turn dangerous, but I stood my ground and demanded our money back. A couple of the men started walking towards us, but thankfully, two security guards from the resort intervened. They were aware of the scam and retrieved our money, warning us that it wasn't safe to confront locals outside the resort. We had dodged a bullet, but the experience reinforced my hatred of injustice and my intolerance of being ripped off. It was an eye-opener to the realities of the wider world, far removed from Thurso. Despite that encounter, the rest of our holiday went smoothly, and we had an amazing time. Jamaica was incredible and an eye-opener.

Once the holiday ended, we returned to Thurso, but my perspective had changed. I had glimpsed the wider world and the opportunities beyond. Upon arriving home, I decided my time in Thurso had come to an end. I wanted to leave behind my friends, the Kuk Sool class I had worked so hard to build, and the life I had established. In later years, I realised this urge to leave was part of the psychological aftermath of being brought up in care and enduring trauma. Deep down, you often feel undeserving of happiness or acceptance, and self-sabotage becomes a recurring theme in adulthood. If only I had understood this back then, I could have avoided so much pain.

One day, I woke up and decided to apply to either Glasgow or Edinburgh to continue my studies in health, fitness, and sports science. I applied and attended interviews in both cities. During the physical tests, I excelled, outperforming everyone. In Edinburgh, one of the instructors noted that the highest abdominal bleep test score ever recorded had been level nine, but I kept going until he stopped me at level eleven. At that point, I was doing one or two thousand sit-ups a week, and my training partners were used to the insane intensity I demanded. I returned home and waited for the results. Eventually, I was notified that I had been accepted to study in Edinburgh. My girlfriend and I discussed it, and she agreed to move with me to start a new life there. A friend of hers had a flat on Gorgie Road, right across from the football stadium, and we planned to move in.

We arrived on a Saturday, coinciding with a big football match. As soon as I stepped out of the car, I realised how different it was from the small towns I had known. I hated crowds at the best of times, and this was overwhelming. We moved into the top-floor flat, and thus began the next chapter of my journey. After a week or so, I started to settle into life in Edinburgh. We were busy painting and moving in our belongings, gradually adapting to city life. One of the first strange things we noticed was a woman living in the top-floor flat opposite ours. Every day, she stood completely naked at her window, entirely unbothered. We definitely weren't in Thurso anymore.

I started my studies and applied for a bursary to support myself financially. Meanwhile, my girlfriend began job hunting. Times were tough; we had no money at all – we had to go to the bank to withdraw our last five pounds in order to buy a bag of potatoes, which would be our food for the next few days until my bursary arrived. This was long before food banks, and I would rather have gone hungry than accept charity. It just wasn't in my nature to take something I hadn't earned, no matter the cost.

Eventually, my partner found a job in a clothing store on Princes Street, and things began to stabilise. I persevered with my studies, though I found it challenging due to my negative experiences in school. Later, I needed to do some work experience, so I approached a gym a couple of miles from our flat. It was called Bodytalk Health and Fitness Centre, owned by a lady named Paula and her daughter, Nicky Bell.

I started working the morning shift, opening up the gym at 7 am. Every day, I would get up at half-past five and walk an hour to the gym, regardless of the weather. It was a lovely little gym with a family feel, and the staff were close-knit, and looking out for each other. We had such a great laugh together, which made work so much more enjoyable. I loved conducting fitness assessments for clients and creating workout and diet plans to help them get into shape. It brought me great joy to see people transform into better versions of themselves, both physically and mentally.

During this period, Master Gavin Chung moved to Edinburgh to study. I got in touch with him, and we began training together in Kuk Sool. Every Saturday, he would come over to my flat, and we would spend a few hours perfecting our martial arts techniques. Eventually, I realised we needed more space, so I approached the owner of Bodytalk about starting Kuk Sool Won classes there, and she agreed. For the first year, it was mostly just

Gavin and me training, with the occasional person joining us but often dropping out.

One day, a reporter from a prominent Edinburgh newspaper spotted me training in the local park. I was practising jump kicks, acrobatics, and martial arts moves, and he asked if he could write a story about my martial art style. I mentioned that I was running classes, so he wrote the piece and included a photo of me performing an impressive vertical roundhouse kick. At our next class, thirty people showed up, and just like that, Edinburgh Kuk Sool Won was born. It was the third Kuk Sool school to open in Scotland, following Thurso and Wick, which I had started alongside my instructor, Master Martin. At that time, there were no other Kuk Sool schools in Scotland, and as the only black belt and highest-ranked practitioner, I was mostly left to train and develop on my own. That suited me well, as I never had any trouble motivating myself.

I was in full work mode, determined to move forward in life. On study days, I focused on my education, and on workdays, I gave my all at the gym. It was a tough routine. A typical day involved waking up at half-past five, working at the gym until three, walking home to relax for an hour, then tackling any homework before heading to class from six to nine. After class, I would walk back home, getting in at ten, and then work on assessments or any other tasks until midnight or later. It was a gruelling schedule, but I was driven and focused.

Our hard work paid off, and we managed to buy a flat in the Slateford area of Edinburgh. It was an older, rundown place, which was all we could afford, but we put in the effort to make it nice. Between work, studies, and renovating the flat, I had my hands full, but eventually, our one-bedroom flat looked great and felt like home.

Master gavin chung and myself early days training bodytalk gym in Edinburgh

Kicking practise with one of my students

Off the wall roundhouse kick with master gavin

Me with my first grand champion trophy

CHAPTER 12:
PUSHING MY LIMITS

After breakdancing had declined around 1986, I had channelled my energy into Kuk Sool. However, in Edinburgh, breakdancing began to make a big comeback in the mid-90s, which made me very happy. I had loved the creativity and sense of freedom that breakdancing brought, as well as the discipline of working tirelessly to master new moves. I started dancing again around 1995 or 1996, attending a local hip-hop night at a club in Edinburgh called Scratch. The DJs were fantastic, and there was a lively breakdance scene there. Every night, there would be a dance battle, where breakdancers formed a circle, each taking turns to showcase their best moves in a highly competitive, almost tribal setting. It was all about earning respect, and you had to be genuinely good to survive in the circle.

I thrived on the challenge of battling and took on anyone willing to step up. One night, the promoter noticed me dominating the dance circle and asked if I wanted to become the resident breakdancer for the club nights. It wasn't a paid gig, but I got free entry to all the big nights, and I couldn't resist the chance to dance regularly, so I agreed. This role introduced me to even more breakdancers. During this time, I met an old-school breakdancer from Elgin named Jim. He had been around when my original breakdance crew used to compete, so we already knew each other. Jim had since moved to Edinburgh, and we decided to form a new breakdance crew and train together, attending jams and events.

I was back doing what I loved, training hard every day, perfecting head spins, and inventing unique moves that no one had ever seen or could replicate. It was a creative outlet that also complemented my martial arts practice. Meanwhile, I competed regularly in UK championships, winning numerous gold medals each year and eventually earning my second UK Grand Champion title at second dahn.

I was now both a first and second dahn Grand Champion, at the top of my game. By then, I was dancing at many venues, and my phone was constantly ringing with people wanting me to perform at their shows or gigs. We had started dancing at Henry's Cellar Bar in Edinburgh on Tuesday nights. The DJs who played there would later become world mixing champions, so there was a lot of talent in that place - breakdancers, MCs, and DJs alike. We would even occasionally meet famous people who dropped in from time to time.

When I danced at Scratch, I often didn't get home until around 3 am on early Sunday morning. Despite that, I still had to open the gym on Sundays, meaning I only got about two hours of sleep. My body was regularly sore from the flips and intense moves of the night before, combined with my Kuk Sool training and studies. I was pushing myself too hard, and eventually, something had to give - and it did. My health suffered as a result. Even though I was in incredible shape, with every muscle defined and in peak physical condition, I woke up one morning with a rash running down my side and felt like I had the worst flu imaginable. I felt absolutely dreadful.

I went to the doctor, who diagnosed me with shingles. I'd never heard of it before, and he explained that it was similar to adult chickenpox, brought on by extreme stress or exhaustion. Essentially, I had run myself into the ground, and my body couldn't cope. The rash cleared up within two weeks, but the post-viral fatigue was severe - like the worst hangover you could ever imagine, multiplied by ten. I was utterly shattered and felt miserable. It was a wake-up call: you can't push yourself beyond your physical limits indefinitely.

Determined to recover, I bought a juicer and started drinking huge glasses of freshly juiced fruit and vegetables. I threw in everything that had health benefits, especially anything green, even if it tasted revolting. At the time, I was a committed vegetarian and had been for many years, believing firmly in the power of good, wholesome food over processed rubbish. I also didn't drink alcohol and was focused on taking quality supplements. I realised I had to ease back on some of my activities.

The recovery process took about a year before I began to feel like myself again. During that time, I prioritised my health rather than pushing myself relentlessly. Gradually, as I got better, I started training again, rebuilding my fitness bit by bit. It was a long, tough battle. Even when I felt awful, I kept dancing because it was my passion. As my health improved, more and more breakdance gigs came my way.

One memorable opportunity was performing for Prince Charles at Holyrood Palace, at a gathering he was hosting with other well-known guests. I agreed, and it was the second time I had the honour of performing for the future king - the first being as a martial artist and now as a breakdancer. The symmetry of this struck me as significant, symbolising my two great passions: martial arts and dance, my yin and yang. After the performance, I had a chance to speak with Prince Charles. I reminded him about the honorary Kuk Sool black belt he received in Thurso, and we talked about some of the moves I had done. He remarked on how difficult they looked, which felt like another small piece of validation fitting into the jigsaw puzzle of my life.

Despite this, I knew deep in my heart that no matter what I achieved or how far I went, it would never feel like enough. I was searching for something intangible and unachievable, a relentless drive born from my past. It's a tough reality, knowing you are driven and focused on reaching a destination you can never truly arrive at. It feels like a curse, but it's something over which I have no control. It's just how I am - or, more accurately, what happened to me in my younger years shaped me into this person.

About a year after recovering from post-viral fatigue, which had been rough, I faced my next health scare. One

Friday, I woke up thinking I had trapped wind. I was in pain all day and couldn't sleep that night. By Saturday, the pain persisted, but I went to teach a three-hour, high-intensity class. Throughout, I felt unwell, with a stabbing pain in my lower abdomen. I dismissed it, having a high pain tolerance. By Monday, the pain had not subsided, so I went to see my GP. He examined me and said it was a torn muscle. I told him I had torn plenty of muscles over the years from breakdancing and martial arts, and this didn't feel the same. He advised me to rest and come back if it didn't improve.

A couple of nights later, the pain was still unbearable. My partner and I went to the video store, but I had to go outside and sit on the ground because the pain was so severe. That night, I was up again, doubled over in agony. The next day, I made an emergency appointment with the doctor. As soon as he saw me, he said I needed to go to hospital immediately. I asked, "When?" and "What for?" He replied, "Now. You have acute appendicitis." I asked if I could go home first to grab a few things, but he insisted I couldn't. He was about to call an ambulance when I mentioned that my partner had a car and could drive me there.

Once at the hospital, they took my blood and measured my oxygen levels. The nurse asked if I was holding my breath. I said no, and she explained that my breaths were very long and slow. I told her I had extreme anxiety and used breath control and meditation to slow my heart rate, especially during high-stress situations - like this one. Health had been my nemesis, and the fear of dying young caused me immense stress. The surgeon came in and told me I needed surgery straight away; there was no time to wait. I turned to my partner and said, "I'll see you after the surgery," and then I was wheeled away.

I was under anaesthetic and oblivious to what was happening, but my partner was told to call an hour later for an update. When she did, I was still in surgery, which worried her. It turned out that my appendix had been leaking, and I was gravely ill. The operation took much longer than expected as the surgeons struggled to locate and remove the appendix. Eventually, they managed to control the situation, but I was left with a large scar across my side. I later learned that my brother George had experienced something similar. I had survived, but the doctors said that if I'd waited a few more hours, it could have killed me. After the operation, I developed a severe infection and was coughing up green mucus. My immune system had taken another major hit.

This experience made me realise how close I had come to death, and that my stubbornness had nearly cost me my life. Recovery from the surgery was slow, with the nine-inch scar taking about a year to heal fully. It was difficult for me to slow down, but I had no choice. During this challenging time, I had to accept that I wasn't invincible. However, I knew that exercise and martial arts were crucial to my recovery, so I gradually rebuilt my strength - both physically and mentally.

My mental strength has been linked to my physical activity. When I train hard, I can manage my spiralling, catastrophic thoughts to some extent, but the mental battle is exhausting. It requires constant vigilance over my thoughts, every second of every day.

Once I regained my strength, I returned to breakdancing, performing at shows all over the UK and attending most of the breakdance and hip-hop nights in Edinburgh and Glasgow. It felt like being fifteen again, rediscovering my first love. Kuk Sool Edinburgh was thriving, with many talented students and a high standard of practice. I was at my peak, both physically and mentally, and immersed myself in the physical demands of my training. Yet, I was unaware that I was merely burying my past traumas.

The sad reality for survivors of childhood trauma is the belief that by pushing memories deep down, we have them under control. But the subconscious has a way of bringing unresolved trauma to the surface, forcing us to address it, as I would later learn. We may think we're bulletproof, but the body keeps score, letting us know when something is wrong. Healing requires recognising that there is a problem. This is the insidious nature of trauma: we can only suppress it temporarily. Real recovery demands painful soul-searching and an admission of our struggles, both to ourselves and to those who care about us. Without that, we can never truly start to heal.

Looking back now, I can see things so much more clearly, as if a veil has been lifted. I only wish I'd realised this in my twenties rather than in my fifties, saving myself so much pain. But that's hindsight for you; we all wish we could go back and change something. I now understand that even our pain provides life lessons. No matter how difficult, we learn from both the good and the bad - though some lessons are harder than others.

It's strange, but even when things are going well, I have an internal urge to destroy what I've built. Stability feels suffocating, like a weight on my chest, and I get the overwhelming need to run away and start afresh. By the time I was living in Edinburgh, this feeling had resurfaced. As I entered my thirties, I wanted to reset my life. It's hard to explain, but the struggle of having nothing seems ingrained in me, and the process of rebuilding and overcoming adversity is part of my DNA. I've had it explained to me why people with CPTSD behave this way.

I loved my time at Bodytalk, and teaching martial arts was a huge part of my life. Yet, the urge to destroy the stability I'd worked so hard to achieve became overpowering. It's a self-destructive cycle that I've repeated many times. It's painful to look back at the people I've let down or the hearts I've broken, but when you live with CPTSD, trust me, you have no control over it. It's how childhood abuse shaped me, and it has cost me dearly. I've tried to be a kind and caring person, but tearing down everything I've achieved only reinforced the self-loathing and hatred I felt towards myself. In those moments, it's as if I'm transported back to being a scared six-year-old in the coal bunker, feeling that everyone hates me, that I'm worthless and unworthy of anything. The feelings are soul-crushing. That's the cruelty of CPTSD: it distorts your self-image to the point where you loathe your own existence, feeling that the world would be better off without you.

By now, I had entered my thirties. My twenties had been full of success and achievements, but my mind couldn't register any of it. I had left my hometown and moved to Edinburgh, becoming the first-ever Scottish black belt in my martial art and the first Scot to win UK Grand Champion at both first dahn and second dahn. I had completed my education, a huge accomplishment given how difficult school had been for me. I had established three of the first Kuk Sool Won schools in Scotland and was in the process of opening a fourth in Glasgow. I had performed Kuk Sool demonstrations for Prince Charles and Prince Edward, and I had hosted the Grandmaster's first-ever visit to my schools in Thurso and Edinburgh.

I became the gym manager at Bodytalk and founded a highly successful personal training business. I was even offered a prestigious job in Dubai, working as a personal trainer for a luxury car brand, but I turned it down to keep teaching and spreading the art of Kuk Sool Won. I had been featured in national martial arts magazines and wrote an article on advanced stretching for one of them. I appeared on TV several times for both martial arts and breakdancing, participating in various news features and segments. I had done promotional dance work for big brands like Red Bull, Nike, and Levi's, and I had met quite a few celebrities along the way. I had also performed alongside hip-hop artists from both the UK and the USA, who I had idolised growing up, at club nights in Edinburgh and Glasgow.

One of my favourite appearances was on *The Live Floor Show*, hosted by Greg Hemphill from *Chewin' the Fat* and *Still Game* on the BBC. Spending the day filming was incredible. There were different comedians doing sketches, including Frankie Boyle. I played an old man on crutches who goes to a faith healer. The healer lays hands on my head, declares me "healed," and I throw away the crutches, launching into backflips and head spins. It was a fantastic experience, observing the behind-the-scenes work at the BBC and seeing how a sketch show is made.

By anyone else's standards, my twenties were packed with personal achievements. But my mind couldn't accept any of it. Listing these accomplishments feels as though I'm talking about someone else, reporting their successes rather than my own. I'm so detached from it. Instead, I only focus on the failures, the times I fell short or let people down, never allowing myself a moment's respite from my relentless self-criticism. I constantly reinforced my own mental punishment. Despite everything, I still felt that I wasn't enough. I'm not even sure what I'm searching for, but nothing seems to satisfy that drive for acceptance and recognition. It's not about proving how good I am, as it was in my youth, but rather proving that I matter - that I'm not the worthless piece of rubbish I was told I was. Those words, burned into my brain from a young age, have left deep scars.

Yes, I'm searching for the unsearchable - a cruel punishment that life has given me, which will remain with me every second of every day until I pass to the other side. It's so difficult to live with. My best friend and training partner at the time often commented on how I would say, "When I achieve this or gain that in life, I'll have made it." Yet, whenever I did achieve or gain those things, I would move the goalposts, setting an even harder, more unattainable target for myself to strive and struggle for. I now realise that the struggle had become my identity and where I felt normal, for lack of a better word. It's difficult to describe, and I don't fully understand it myself, but it's always there, weighing heavy on my soul like a million tons.

Bruce lee was my hearo and i trained to look just like him
Training to the max everyday peak fitness

CHAPTER 13:

ALL CHANGE, JAYS ARRIVAL

As time went on and my twenties slipped away, my CPTSD began to overwhelm me. The urge to run away and start over again burned deep within me, and I felt suffocated by the routine of my life. Imagine feeling an overpowering urge to destroy everything you've worked so hard to achieve, just as you start to feel successful or content. After about a year of battling this feeling in my head, I finally decided it was time to leave the long-term relationship I had been in for over twelve years. I knew it would be painful and hurt the people involved, but CPTSD is a relentless force, dominating and controlling a sufferer's actions. The feeling that I didn't deserve a stable, loving home overwhelmed me, so I made the difficult decision to move on and start again.

The urge for self-destruction is strange. It drives you to tear down everything you've built, regardless of the cost. Looking back, it breaks my heart, as I didn't know what CPTSD was or how it affected me. I thought I was just messed up. So, I moved out of the flat in Edinburgh that I had worked so hard on with my partner, and I moved in with a friend from Glasgow. He lived in a fairly rough area, a stark contrast to the quiet street I'd lived on in Edinburgh. It was a difficult time, starting from scratch once more. Due to unforeseen circumstances, I lost all the money from the sale of the flat, and I was left broke, living in my friend's flat in Glasgow. Talk about self-sabotage - but this was me; this was the way my past had shaped me.

I was still teaching my classes in Edinburgh, so four times a week I would take the train. Money was tight, so I walked to the station in Glasgow, took the train, and then walked to the training hall in Edinburgh. The whole journey took about two hours each way, which was far from ideal, but I had no choice.

Once again, I found myself in that familiar place of self-loathing, hatred, and the feeling that I had ruined everything. The most painful part was that my actions hurt others. I had a habit of suddenly walking away from friendships and relationships, waking up one day and deciding it was over, needing to start a new life to quieten my mind and ease my anxiety.

There was an overwhelming, crushing feeling deep inside me, and somehow, I found comfort in pain, loss, and self-loathing. It's hard to explain - try living in my brain for an hour, let alone a day or a year. It's exhausting.

Years later, my counsellor told me, "You must find it really tiring." She felt drained after our sessions, and I replied, "Imagine having that every second of every day until you fall asleep." And I sleep very little - six hours is a long sleep for me, with most nights averaging four or five. The slightest sound or movement snaps me awake, ready to fight some imaginary threat. Then, I slowly realise there is no threat, and I try to go back to sleep. It's a lasting legacy of the past. I replay scenarios in my head, over-analysing every word said to me, searching for hidden meanings or perceived slights. Too many thoughts can wear you out mentally, but that's my life. What a price to pay for the hatred of someone who should have cared for us but didn't.

I often ask myself if I'm angry about all this, and I've come to the conclusion that I'm not angry - I'm heartbroken. I mourn the life I could have had without the abuse, without the self-sabotage, without letting down the people who loved and cared for me, without the constant ruminations and feeling of impending doom. I think about a life without the street fights, conflicts, CPTSD, and FND. But as I've entered my fifties, I've realised that perhaps the universe gave me these challenges for a reason: to endure, to learn, and to heal. It's as though the universe has said, "Your life won't be easy, but it will be worthwhile."

Reflecting on the people I've helped - whether through martial arts, dance, or personal training - I understand now that my desire to help came from a place of pain, suffering, and hardship. Has it been a gift? I'm not sure I can see it that way yet, but I hope to one day. Since starting this journey of self-discovery with the help of my counsellor and other professionals, I'm heartbroken that it's taken me this long to realise that my experiences weren't normal and that I needed to address the pain from the inside out. For years, I tried to shield myself by building a strong, impenetrable body, hoping to ward off the outside world.

But it took years to understand that the damage was already inside me, lurking in the shadows of my mind. No amount of push-ups or training could fix that.

The journey of healing from childhood trauma is the toughest battle I have ever fought, and it's one I will continue until my last breath on this planet. The strangest part is that people often saw me as a machine, bulletproof through martial arts and physical conditioning. But that was just a plaster over a deep, gaping wound that I had never truly addressed.

Life in Glasgow was eventful, filled with nights out partying every weekend and the occasional street fight when I found myself in the wrong place at the wrong time. This chaotic pattern defined my life. During this period, I started a breakdancing company that provided lessons to inner-city youth from deprived areas who had endured tough circumstances. I found this work incredibly rewarding and close to my heart. Over the years, I completed hundreds of teaching jobs in some of Glasgow's roughest areas, knowing that breakdancing could be a way for these young people to escape their hardships. We connected on a meaningful level; I understood them, and they understood me. My company was busy, and I was able to give work to other breakdancers in the area. I put in long hours and a lot of travel, doing one of the most physically demanding jobs imaginable: backflipping and spinning on my head all day. By the time I got home each night, I was battered and exhausted, but I gave 100% to my teaching.

During this time, I had a couple of girlfriends, but the same pattern repeated: I would be in the relationship for about a year before finding a reason to end it. The familiar cycle of pushing people away whenever they got too close dominated my personal life. It wasn't the fault of the women I was with; it was the suffocating feeling I had - that deep-seated sense that I didn't deserve love or happiness. It's hard to describe, but it felt like a profound guilt and shame, like a scar on my soul that no one could see but that I could always feel. I never talked about it with anyone. This self-destructive cycle of breaking up and starting over controlled me.

Despite this, I was driven and focused on creating success. By the time I turned thirty-three, I realised I wanted something more permanent. I needed a relationship that would last, rather than the short-term flings that usually ended in heartache. I started to recognise that I was in a self-destructive loop, and I wondered how I would ever find happiness if I kept sabotaging it.

That's the all-consuming power of trauma from childhood abuse. It leaves a lasting impact. I wanted to become a father and provide the love and protection I never had. Around this time, I started chatting with a girl named Pauline. We connected online, exchanging messages every few days, just normal chit-chat about how our days had been. After about a year, we finally agreed to meet in person. She worked at a tool hire company in Edinburgh but lived in Falkirk. We went on a date and hit it off immediately, speaking every day after that. We became inseparable. I felt she was the one. At thirty-three, I needed more from life, and Pauline felt like my soulmate. We had so much in common, and she understood me in a way no one else had. She was great fun, a bit wild, and loved to party, but she was also one of the kindest, most caring people I had ever met. Pauline had a fiery side and knew how to stand up for herself, which only strengthened our connection.

We met in July 2003, and by December, she was pregnant. It might sound quick, but it was planned. I knew if anyone should be the mother of my child, it was Pauline. So, we let nature take its course, and five months later, she was pregnant. At the time, I was staying at a friend's house in Glasgow, sharing his spare room, while Pauline lived with her dad. It probably wasn't the best time to plan for a child, but I was determined to make it work and provide a good life for our new family. Shortly after, I moved in with Pauline and her dad, sharing her room while I worked to get back on my feet and find us a place in Falkirk. I was constantly travelling between Edinburgh and Falkirk, teaching martial arts classes, running breakdance workshops, and doing personal fitness training. It was a physically demanding and exhausting schedule.

As Jay's due date approached, I promised myself that I would give my son the life I had dreamed of. It was my chance to right the wrongs of the past and make things better. This was the most important mission of my life, and I couldn't afford to fail. On the day of Jay's birth, my anxiety was through the roof. My brain was racing with countless "what if" scenarios. I felt dizzy and nauseous as I waited outside the delivery room, overwhelmed by the significance of the moment. All my hopes and dreams were about to become real, and I was determined to protect Jay from the harshness of the world. I wanted him to see only kindness, love, and care - the complete opposite of what I had experienced.

A nurse finally called out, "You can come in, Mr Mackenzie." My legs felt like they were about to give way from nerves. When I walked into the room, I saw Pauline's face and the doctors working around her as she was having a C-section. The song *Mrs Robinson* was playing, which felt surreal. I sat next to Pauline, told her I loved her, and reassured her that everything would be okay. The fear, excitement, and nerves were overwhelming. My heart was pounding, my mouth was dry, and I struggled to speak, but Pauline was calm and focused.

Jay was in the breech position, so they delivered him via C-section. The first glimpse I had of him was when the doctors took him over to the table to clean him up. He was perfect, absolutely beautiful. I was speechless. Pauline and I had created this incredible little human being. As I tried to stand up, the room started spinning like a fairground ride. I felt the weight of all my past trauma crashing down on me. The emotions, the memories, and the responsibility were overwhelming. I said I needed to go to the toilet as I thought I might pass out. All the feelings I had buried for so long came flooding back. My legs gave way, and the room spun faster and faster. My CPTSD was in overdrive, with a thousand worries and thoughts racing through my mind. Poor Pauline had just given birth, and there I was, about to collapse.

The nurse grabbed a chair for me, and I sat down, feeling sick and faint. It wasn't my proudest moment. I had wanted to be strong for Pauline, but my brain just couldn't handle it. The next thing I knew, I was being wheeled into a bed next to her. We laugh about it now. When I started coming back to my senses, I found myself lying beside Pauline. The nurse brought in tea and toast, and Pauline assumed it was for her, but it was actually for me. I don't remember any of it clearly, but it's funny now.

So, there I was, in a bed next to Pauline, sipping tea and feeling overwhelmed. All the times I'd been in fights, sparring sessions, and martial arts competitions, and the thing that knocked me out was the birth of my son, Jay Mackenzie, on the 9th of September 2004.

A few hours after Jay's birth, a nurse was doing her checks on him. She left and returned with a doctor, and they both began examining Jay. I knew immediately that something was wrong - my brain was hard-wired to detect any signs of trouble. They told us that Jay was struggling to breathe and had to be taken to intensive care. The worry for me and Pauline was indescribable. Pauline had just gone through surgery to bring Jay into the world, and now we were faced with this terrifying situation. The panic we felt was soul-destroying, like being punched in the gut. I tried to stay strong for Pauline, but inside, my heart was pounding out of my chest.

The next few days were some of the toughest of our lives. I wasn't allowed to stay in the hospital overnight, so I had to go home each evening, leaving Pauline to cope on her own until the next visiting hours. She had to get up every few hours to check on Jay, who was hooked up to machines, and I felt completely helpless. Every time I visited, I could see the exhaustion and stress etched on Pauline's face, and there was nothing I could do to make things better. We just had to wait and pray that Jay's heart rate would stabilise and his breathing would improve. After many tears and endless worry, Jay began to get better. Progress was slow but steady, and eventually, he was well enough to come home. The relief we felt was immense. We couldn't wait to leave the hospital, even though the doctors and nurses had been incredible. We were just desperate to start our life together as a family.

On the last day, one of the nurses noticed that I hadn't picked Jay up at all. She asked me about it, and I explained that he seemed so tiny and fragile. Gently, she lifted him and placed him in my arms. The feeling of love and connection I experienced was indescribable. To this day, I have never felt anything even close to that moment. It was absolute perfection - everything I had ever searched for wrapped up in one tiny, beautiful bundle of love: my son.

Back at Pauline's dad's house in March 2004, we were still living in her childhood bedroom. Her dad had been incredibly kind to let us stay, and I am forever grateful for his support. Pauline's sister, Michelle, had decorated the spare room to make a nursery for Jay. Life was finally moving in the right direction for our little family. It was a steep learning curve, especially since I'd never really held a baby before. Changing nappies was a particular challenge for me - I would gag and nearly vomit every time - but I soon adapted to life as a dad. I'd get up in the middle of the night to feed Jay, then start my fourteen-hour teaching days at 6 am. It was tough, but I cherished every second I spent with Jay.

Around that time, Pauline's family dog, Meg, gave birth to a litter of puppies. I was there to watch them being born, and as a lifelong dog lover, it was an unforgettable experience. Sadly, one of the pups struggled from the start and, despite our efforts to care for him around the clock, he passed away. It broke my heart. One of the other pups wasn't taken, so Pauline and I adopted her and named her Pip. She became the love of my life, and we were inseparable. Pip was my first dog since Rusty from the children's home, and the bond we shared was unique. I found it easier to accept unconditional love from a dog than from a human, and Pip's presence brought me comfort. She was by my side, never more than a few inches away, and she gave me the kind of love I could accept without question.

Throughout my life, I've had a deep connection to animals, especially dogs. I think it's the loyalty and unconditional love they give that resonates with me. But I hadn't had a dog since Rusty, the dog from the children's home. The way I found out about Rusty's death on April 1st shattered me, and I vowed never to go through the pain of losing a dog again.

It's one of life's lessons, isn't it? We're gifted these four-legged companions who bring us joy and love, but in exchange, we must endure the agony of losing them. That pain is the price of understanding the value of pure, unconditional love.

Then along came Pip. She was the second dog in my life, and I was there when she was born. I was the first to pick her up and hold her. At the time, she was the only pup in the litter no one had chosen, but she turned out to be the most special. Pip was a black bearded collie with a loving personality, and from the moment we brought her home, she became a daddy's girl. We were soulmates, inseparable. Pip was SO pure, and I believe she was sent from the other side to teach me about unconditional love. She truly was amazing

I was working six days a week, pushing hard to secure a more permanent home for our family. It was a period of relentless hard work, driven by my determination to ensure that Jay never had to struggle as I had. I was prepared to do whatever it took to protect him from life's hardships. This was a challenging time for both me and Pauline. It was all work and graft, but the reward was the precious moments we shared with Jay and Pip. Those family times were incredible.

Jay was a light sleeper, just like his dad. The slightest noise would wake him, and he'd be up crying for hours. We tiptoed around the house like ninjas, trying to keep the peace. In his first couple of years, Jay had several hospital stays. His temperature would spike, and he'd struggle to breathe, forcing us to rush him to hospital. The worry was excruciating. With my overactive, ruminating mind, I struggled to cope, and panic would take over. All my hopes and dreams were tied to my son, and it broke me to see him struggling. Eventually, he was diagnosed with asthma. As a baby, he seemed allergic to the world, and it was a constant battle to manage work, make ends meet, and save for the future.

146

My beautiful soul mate Pip. I miss her everyday.

CHAPTER 14:

BUILDING A LIFE

Eventually, in 2006, we managed to get a council flat in Falkirk, just a five-minute walk from Pauline's dad, which was ideal. Whenever we weren't working, we took turns staying overnight at the new flat, painting and doing DIY to get it ready for us to move into. After some time, we finally settled into our little home. The street was full of mostly good people, but weekends could be wild, with some kind of drama unfolding. Despite that, it was our first home, and we loved it.

We balanced my breakdancing work and classes with Pauline's care job. I'd come home from work, and Pauline would head out for her shifts, meaning we were busy and tired. But it was worth it. My son was beautiful, and I was determined to give him a great life and right the wrongs of the past.

One challenge at the time was cash flow. Although I was busy with breakdancing jobs, getting paid was often a struggle. I had to invoice clients and wait four to six weeks for payments, which meant that even though I was working constantly, we often found ourselves broke. Sometimes, even scraping together money for train fares to get to jobs was difficult. On any given day, I could be in Perth in the morning, Paisley in the afternoon, and Edinburgh at night, which made the cost of public transport very high. We were chasing payments and juggling our finances, but Pauline's regular wage helped keep us afloat until my invoices were paid.

Being a dad to Jay brought me immense joy. For the first time, I felt complete and had a true family of my own. Of course, I still battled daily with my CPTSD, but being so busy helped me keep it under control. The harder I worked, the more I could manage my thoughts and ruminations. Jay gave me a focus and drive to create the best possible life for my family.

Over time, our situation improved, and Pauline decided we needed a family car. We ended up with a heavily modified "boy racer" car, which we bought because we got a great deal on it. It wasn't ideal - it was so lowered that it could barely make it over a speed bump - but it was transport. Our flat had a wonderful atmosphere, and we often had friends over on weekends, relaxing, listening to music, and having fun. One of our closest friends, Amanda, was a regular visitor, and she helped babysit Jay while I worked and Pauline went to her job. Despite the hard work and constant hustle, we created some amazing memories. Those times gave me my first real sense of a normal family life, something I cherished.

That said, things weren't without issues. When I first met Pauline, I hadn't told her anything about my past, not even that I taught martial arts for a living. She knew very little about my childhood, only that my mum and dad had died when I was a baby. My mum passed away when I was two, and later in life, I eventually discovered who my dad was when his daughter - my half-sister - got in touch. For most of my life, I only knew my mum's name; I knew nothing about my father. He'd had an affair with my mum while already having a family of his own. When he found out my mum was pregnant, I believe his wife gave him an ultimatum, and he chose to have no contact with me. I later learned that he once came up to the children's home with my brother George and watched me playing in the front garden, but he never spoke to me. He just said, "That's my son," and then left.

I now realise that I'm nothing like my biological father. There is no situation in which I would ever abandon my son. As an adult, I understand that life is complicated, but it still feels incomprehensible to me. He knew I was in the children's home yet chose to stay away. In my eyes, that was weakness, no matter the circumstances. I only learned all this in my thirties. Up until then, I thought my dad was dead and knew nothing else about him. I often wonder what I'd say if I could go back in time and speak to my parents. I don't hate my dad; he's just nothing to me. He abandoned me and chose his other family, so I've always felt we are fundamentally different.

When Jay was young, these thoughts surfaced more frequently. It was unthinkable to me that I could ever abandon him, especially knowing what I went through in the children's home. The thought of leaving him to that kind of life sent shivers down my spine. I would do anything to protect my son and my family, and all my friends know that my family is my top priority. After Jay was born, I thought a lot about my parents and the choices they made, and how those choices impacted their children.

Pauline eventually noticed that at family gatherings, like parties or Christmas, I would retreat upstairs to our room after an hour or so. Because I hadn't talked about my past, she thought I was being rude. But this behaviour was just part of who I was, and I had no concept of CPTSD or the habits it brings, like avoidance and self-isolation. I didn't understand my overwhelming need to escape and be alone, away from others, to find safety in solitude. Looking back, it's so clear now, but at the time, I just thought that was how I was. Pauline picked up on it even when we were with a room full of friends, realising there was something different about how I interacted with people.

Over time, I began to open up to Pauline, revealing my backstory bit by bit. It took nearly twenty years for me to share everything. There are some things you don't want anyone to know, no matter how close they are. It's a mix of guilt and shame, combined with a feeling that you shouldn't talk about it - that you have to keep it buried to maintain control. But burying trauma only creates more problems. Many people I grew up with never talked about their abuse, even to their partners or spouses. My brother Andrew, for instance, never told his wife or family anything, even though I knew it was taking a huge toll on him. He cut himself off from everyone, just like me, and had no contact with childhood friends. Isolation becomes a way to regulate emotions, but it also robs you of normal relationships with friends and family.

Looking back now, after years of counselling and reading about the causes of both FND and CPTSD, I'm finally starting to understand how destructive these conditions are. The saddest part is that we are often unaware of how deeply our behaviours are rooted in trauma. Realising this breaks my heart a bit, because if I'd known earlier, I could have lived differently and caused less pain to those I loved. I felt an intense awkwardness and discomfort when shown affection. It's hard to explain, but it's a feeling so strong it's almost unbearable.

Life was fairly normal and stable at this point. Work was going really well. By then, I had martial arts schools in Edinburgh and Glasgow and was doing numerous freelance breakdancing jobs across central Scotland. I had worked with various organisations, and at one point, I did some gigs for Rangers FC. Personally, I have zero interest in football, but many of my friends are fans. I had to wear a Rangers tracksuit and accompany a player to a school in inner Glasgow. One of my first gigs was with Charlie Adams, and it was filmed for Sky Sports News. We were also invited to perform breakdancing at the Rangers AGM in front of the entire team. It was a memorable experience, especially when Ally McCoist came over with some of the team for photos. It felt surreal: a boy from the far north of Scotland with a tough start in life, now dancing for Rangers at their AGM. I even invited some of my breakdancing friends who were Rangers fans and brought along my old schoolmate Willie Millar from our Thurso breakdancing crew, the Egyptian Warriors. It was amazing to see how far we'd come from practising head spins in his bedroom as teenagers. It just goes to show that hard work really does pay off.

I worked long hours and also collaborated with a Glasgow-based arts and dance company called Impact Arts. It was during a job for them that I suffered a major setback. On my lunch break, I noticed a springboard in the hall and decided to try a back somersault with a half twist - a move I had done countless times before. I was tired from teaching all morning but went for it anyway. As I landed, I felt a crunch in my knee. Over the years, I've had more sports injuries than I can count, and I usually just pushed through the pain. In the world of martial arts, it was all about showing no weakness and being tough. But this was different; I could barely walk. Worse still, after lunch, I had to teach breakdancing to thirty kids for three hours. I limped through the class and managed to get to the train station, barely able to walk. My knee had swollen up like a balloon, but I convinced myself it would get better in a few days with rest.

I had three days left on the contract, and I'd never cancelled a teaching job before, no matter how bad I felt. People relied on me, so I pushed through. But this time, I had no choice. I couldn't walk, let alone teach, and for the first time ever, I had to cancel. Being self-employed, not working meant not getting paid, and we relied heavily on that income. That weekend, we had a big show on stage in

Glasgow. I hobbled there, and my friends helped cover for me. Thankfully, I was a pretty good body popper, so I managed to stand still and pop while my friends carried me off stage. I knew it was serious, so I went to the doctor. He said I needed an MRI scan, but it would take a couple of months on the NHS. Desperate, I scraped together the money to pay for a private scan, which confirmed that I had torn my cartilage and needed surgery.

Because I had already had the MRI, the wait for my operation wasn't as long. In the meantime, I strapped up my knee and wore a support, doing my best to keep functioning. Not working wasn't an option. Those were painful days, breakdancing on a torn knee, but needs must. I eventually had the surgery and was told to stay off my knee for twelve weeks. Two weeks after the operation, I did a Kuk Sool testing I needed to complete in order to stay on track for my master testing. I took it slowly and steadily, working every day to rehabilitate my knee and rebuild my strength. It was tough going. I was used to leaping around doing backflips and jump kicks, but that had to stop. It took about a year before I could function relatively normally again, but the damage was significant, and I had to modify many of the things I used to do. Still, I found ways to adapt. I have never been one to give up and believed that hard work could fix almost anything.

By then, I was approaching my forties and realised I needed to be more sensible. I eventually sold my Glasgow martial arts class to another instructor. Travelling to Glasgow every night, after already commuting all over central Scotland during the day, was taking up too much time. I was spending at least three to four hours on trains and buses, so I decided to open a martial arts class in Falkirk to be closer to home and spend more time with Jay. By that point, I had opened schools in Thurso, Wick, Edinburgh, Glasgow, Paisley, and now Falkirk. Kuk Sool had spread significantly, and many of the current instructors came from my schools. By then, I had been teaching for over twenty years and was on my way to becoming the first-ever Scottish master of the Korean martial art I practised.

I had won International Martial Art School of the Year with EFC twice, beating schools from across the UK and America. EFC, or Educational Funding Company, was one of the largest martial arts billing companies at the time, and winning the Fastest Growing School in my division came with a £1,000 prize each time, which was a huge help. I had also travelled extensively, both teaching and training, including a trip to Houston, Texas. I hate flying, ever since my first thirteen-hour flight to Jamaica, but Pauline booked everything for me because I needed to complete the final part of my testing to achieve master rank - a goal that had taken twenty-five years of daily practice to reach.

Pauline booked and paid for the flight, telling me I was going whether I liked it or not. I gave myself a couple of months to get in peak physical condition and sharpen up on the hundreds of self-defence techniques I needed to demonstrate during the all-day testing. As the day drew closer, I felt ready and in peak form. I flew to the States, determined to achieve my lifelong dream of becoming the first Scottish Kuk Sool Won master. Thinking back to the kid I was when I first stepped into Master Martin's school in Halesworth, it was incredible to see how far I'd come. All the sacrifices, years of training, and dedication had paid off.

It was a long way from being that frightened little boy, locked in the cupboard or shivering on the dark stairs, or washing in the River Thurso after workouts because the place I lived had no running water. Years later, I painted the words "NO EXCUSES" on the wall of my martial arts school as a reminder of my past and a motivation for the future. No one knew anything about my past; they just saw the martial arts machine I had become. It was my way of trying to fix the broken pieces of myself, but no amount of training could undo what had happened in my childhood. I couldn't travel back in time, so transforming myself into a machine was the next best thing.

Earning my fifth-dahn black belt and becoming a master was another huge milestone ticked off my bucket list. Houston was amazing. I even visited the Space Center, which was a dream come true for me. I had been fascinated by space and the universe since childhood, so seeing

Mission Control - the same one I had watched in footage of the Apollo missions - was surreal.

The testing day itself was one of the hardest I'd ever experienced, thanks to the heat in Houston. For the first time, I nearly vomited during a testing session. Usually, I was so fit that I could breeze through them, even though they were gruelling. Over the years, I'd faced incredibly tough testings from American masters, which included hundreds of kicks, push-ups, forms, self-defence techniques, breakfalls, board breaking, and sparring, often lasting all day. My instructor, Master Martin, and Ali pushed me to be better than the day before, instilling a "never quit" attitude in me.

I completed the testing and was told I would be promoted back in the UK. I asked if the promotion could take place in Scotland, as that was incredibly important to me.

Me winning EFC International Martial Arts School of the year

Breakdancing for BBC Blast

CHAPTER 15:

FAMILY

I loved my trip to Houston. It had taken a lifetime of work to reach the master level in Kuk Sool. All the years of hard training, focus, and sacrifice had paid off, and what an achievement it was: the first-ever Scottish Kuk Sool master.

It's hard for people to understand the effort and sacrifice it takes to reach this level. Upon promotion to master level - after twenty-five-plus years of training - you are presented with a white belt, symbolising the full circle back to where you began all those years ago. The only difference is that the master-level white belt is twice as thick as the one you started with. That moment of promotion, back in Scotland, was extraordinary - truly the culmination of a lifetime of hard work.

During this time, I felt an overwhelming urge to uncover where I came from and learn about my family's past. When I was younger, I'd been told no one knew anything about it, but I've always been the type of person who, when I don't understand something, researches it obsessively until I do. So, I decided I would uncover everything I could about my family history. Too many years had passed without knowing where I was from or to whom I belonged.

I began researching my family tree and enlisted the help of an expert in the field. That decision started a journey that would eventually lead me to uncover everything I hadn't known as a child. I found photographs of my mum, my grandparents, and even my great-grandparents. I also tracked down their graves and visited them to connect with my past.

This journey turned out to be deeply painful, and looking back, it had a significant impact on my life. But at the time, I felt compelled to see it through.

As I mentioned earlier, my mum died of cancer when I was just two, and my dad wanted nothing to do with me. As you can imagine, this was a difficult way to start life - not knowing anything about your mum or dad. Fundamentally, as humans, I think we need our parents, and not having them affects everything.

It's hard to describe what it's like slowly realising you're different from the other kids around you. You've lost your parents, and you're being brought up in a care home. To you, it's just your normal life, but gradually, it dawns on you that you are different. Then, a deep longing for a normal family life sets in. Growing up in the home, disappointment becomes your normal. I often dreamed of what it would be like to spend just one day as part of a normal, loving family with a mum and dad, but I have no idea what that feels like. My brain simply can't relate.

Having my own family now is the closest I will ever get, but it's not the same as having unconditional love and support at a young age. It's not the same as having someone there during your darkest moments, telling you that everything will be okay. I think that's what impacted me the most: growing up without that unconditional love from a parent. Now, I would do anything for my son, Jay - anything at all.

Growing up differently meant I was always trying to fit in, but there would be reminders that I didn't - whether at school sports day, Christmas, or moments when I needed someone to acknowledge and be proud of my achievements. Christine and some of the staff at the children's home tried to be there for me, but it wasn't the same. They worked shifts - two days on, two days off - so you wouldn't see them for days at a time.

Much later in life, I found out my mum's name was Andrewena Mackenzie, and she came from Skinnet, in the far north of Scotland. It's a beautiful but remote place, where life was harsh back then. I learned my mum had a very hard life, which broke my heart. She had no money and was raising six children on her own. My mum died aged forty-two, and she'd lost her own mum, Bella Macpherson, when she was around ten. Bella died suddenly in her sleep at the age of thirty-two.

Losing her mum at a young age meant my mum understood the pain of loss. It's strange how the cycle repeated itself with me losing her when I was just two. Losing a parent has a profound impact on your entire life. On top of that, going into a care home and enduring abuse leaves scars that never fully heal.

The man helping me trace my family said it was a tragic story, and I agree. My mum also lost her sister Jessie and Jessie's son, Robert, in a house fire. My grandad accidentally knocked over a Tilley lamp, which set the house on fire. Tragically, Jessie and Robert were in the attic room with no way to escape. Jessie tried to shield her son from the flames, but they both lost their lives. My mum almost died in the fire as well, but she managed to get herself and her other children out. Jessie and Robert weren't so lucky.

Learning about this broke my heart. I often wonder what all this trauma did to my mum's mental health, especially in a time when such things weren't well understood. Finding out about the fire hit me hard. The sheer sadness of it all - the loss, the pain, the tragedy - was overwhelming. Sometimes, uncovering family history can be a double-edged sword. Learning all this sent me into an emotional meltdown. Yet, I'm glad I discovered what my mum had gone through. If she hadn't escaped that fire, I wouldn't be here today.

Weirdly enough, when I was fifty-two, I was on holiday in Thurso, staying at a rented house by the beach. I got chatting to the neighbour next door, who turned out to be from Skinnet, where my family had lived. She suggested I meet her elderly mum, who might remember the fire. I went to meet her, and shockingly, she had lived just up the road from my grandad's house. She had taken my mum and siblings in on the night of the fire.

I couldn't believe it - through a random conversation with a stranger, I had met the woman who gave my family shelter that night. It felt like part of a puzzle I was meant to solve. Speaking with her was incredible, and she even showed me a photo of herself and my auntie Jessie as young girls. Looking back, it's clear how much hardship my mum endured. For me, learning all this was the final straw mentally.

My Complex PTSD (CPTSD) spiralled out of control. It was as if all the trauma had just happened yesterday, and I felt it deeply, as though it were my own. I began waking up feeling emotionally broken, crying over the smallest sad thing I saw on TV. My emotions were completely dysregulated, and I had no control over them.

This was especially hard, as I'd grown up in the seventies, when crying was seen as a weakness. In my care home at the time of Mrs nobody , it was beaten out of you. The more I learned about my past and what my mum and family had gone through, the more my CPTSD worsened. I also developing symptoms of Neurological Disorder (FND). Eventually, I sought help and was officially diagnosed with both conditions.

There were other triggers during this time too. I lost several friends, either to natural causes or suicide. Two of the people who died by suicide had been messaging me beforehand, but I had no idea they were in such pain. Fiona, a girl I worked with on dance jobs, had been seeking advice about a relationship. She spoke to me several times, but one day, I found out through Facebook that she had hanged herself. It was devastating. She was such a kind soul, but life had become too hard for her.

Another loss that hit me hard was my brother George. He was much older than me and hadn't gone into care, so I only met him a handful of times. The last time was at the bus station in Edinburgh. He was a bus driver, and he called out to me. Somehow, he recognised me. He tried to give me some money that day, but I refused. I realise now it was his way of making up for all the birthdays and milestones he'd missed. That was the last time I saw him. When he passed away, I didn't attend the funeral. At the time, I thought it didn't make sense since I barely knew him, but looking back, I wish I'd gone. Hindsight is a funny thing.

George is buried with my mum in Inverness Cemetery. I visit and speak to him there. In time, I've grown closer to his family and now keep in touch with his son, George, his partner, Helen, and his daughter, Tracey.

Reflecting on my life, I see how much CPTSD shaped my thinking. It's like my brain is wired to see the world in black and white - no shades of grey. If someone hurts or betrays me, I shut them out forever. I'm working hard to change this, but it's not easy. Life, after all, isn't black and white. It's messy, complex, and full of shades of grey.

The only picture I have of my mum (digitally restored from original)

Bella, my granny, who died aged 32.
Pauline and I eventually found her grave in Melness Cemetary

My great granny, Christina, with her tea pot at the ready

My mums sister, Jessie, and her son, Robert,
my cousin, who sadly died in the house fire

CHAPTER 16:
SAD DISCOVERIES

I was still teaching breakdancing at this time, working in some of the roughest areas in central Scotland, so there was always some kind of drama. One night, after finishing our teaching for the day, we headed through to Paisley to a friend's house for a barbecue and some downtime. A few of us decided to go to the shop. On the way, a good pal of mine, Johno, who was a brilliant breakdancer, went with two other friends. To get there, they had to pass through a rough scheme.

While walking, a man started shouting abuse at Johno from a block of flats. Johno shouted something back, and before we knew it, the guy came running out of his flat with a knife in his hand. I spotted it straight away and shouted, "Watch out! He's got a blade!" The man ran over to Johno, shouting about us being in his area. Then, without hesitation, he stabbed Johno in the shoulder.

It was the first time I'd seen someone get stabbed. I'd witnessed plenty of violence in my time - fights or being caught up in fights - but never anything like this. I saw the guy slip the knife into the back of his jeans. He started mouthing off at me next, so I confronted him, telling him to throw the knife away and settle it with our fists. Of course, he denied even having a knife, but I knew better. A total coward. I realised he was trying to intimidate me, knowing he was armed, so I called him a chicken-shit bastard and walked away to check on Johno. By that time, Johno was already on his way to the hospital.

Luckily, Johno survived, but it just shows how dangerous the places we ended up could be. Another wild night and a clear case of being in the wrong place at the wrong time. But, as I said, we were always in the roughest areas because that's where we were hired to work, trying to make a difference for young people.

That night was an eye-opener. I was a dad now, and I realised how much worse it could have been. Violence had been a consistent part of my life. I've never walked away when someone tried to put me down or start something, whether it was one person or ten. I have no fear - it was beaten out of me at a young age. It's almost like I constantly test my fear response.

For example, there's a forest behind my house, and you can walk through it to get to town. In winter, it's so pitch black you can't even see your hand in front of your face. There's a path through the trees, and sometimes when I'm walking home in the dark with my phone light on, I turn it off and try to follow the path from memory. I keep going, far past the point where I lose track of the path or risk walking into a tree. I love the sense of the unknown, the challenge of confronting and overcoming my fear of the dark. I know this is a response to my childhood trauma. It's my way of taking control over what once broke me - my dark terror of being alone, of going to bed in the pitch black.

Pauline knows this about me. She's been with me in so many situations and understands that I have zero fear of physical threats. She's seen me fight. She knows I'd never start a fight, but I'd never walk away from one either. I'd rather die than let someone beat me down, no matter the cost. I recognise now that this reaction was instilled in me from a young age, a way of overcoming my perceived weakness.

Having my son, Jay, started to change me at the deepest levels. The unconditional love between a father and his son is something truly special. For Jay, I had limitless love, and I'd do anything to protect him from the hardships of life. That's where my biological father and I are polar opposites. I could never agree with his decision to abandon me. For the first time in my life, I felt a true bond with another soul - a bond with someone who was part of me.

It's strange. I've never been particularly attached to people or places. I've always felt like I don't fit into life, nor do I want to. I know who I am, with all my flaws and failings, but I also know how many people I've helped, motivated, and guided to change their lives.

The strange thing is, as you become more successful, more people start to resent or dislike you. When you succeed, it reminds others of their own struggles and shortcomings. They project their issues onto you. I've never cared about negativity in my life. I had it drummed into me from a young age that I was worthless and beyond love. So, whenever someone disrespects me or takes me for granted, I walk away - no ands, buts, or ifs.

It's one thing I would actually call a benefit of PTSD: the ability to walk away from people who bring drama into your life. Yes, I know it's a trauma response, but I'm grateful for it. It brings closure to the bullshit.

I am always restless, constantly searching for the next challenge or the next thing in my life. Deep inside, I've felt the need to build and create, to strive to become more than the sum of my parts. But this drive has inevitably been counterbalanced by the chaotic force within me - the yin and yang of creation and destruction. The desire to tear down everything positive in my life was often out of control, especially in my forties.

During this time, Jay was young, and I was laser-focused on providing the best life I could for my family. I'd built my martial arts schools into award-winning and successful enterprises. I had a busy personal training company and was still teaching breakdancing. Life was full-on. Yet, deep down, I constantly battled with the belief that I didn't deserve happiness, success, or the love of my family. The mental struggle was relentless, and I wouldn't wish that on anyone. Somehow, though, I was just about holding it all together.

Every night, I would sit in Jay's room before he fell asleep to make sure he knew how much he was loved. I look back now and remember one night when he shouted, "Dada! Dada! There's a monster under my beddie!"

I ran through, looked under his bed, and reassured him that there was no monster. Looking back, it reminded me of when I used to lie in bed, convinced there was a monster under mine. The only difference was that no one came to reassure me. I lay there, terrified, alone with my thoughts. As for monsters? I knew they were real. But they didn't hide under your bed - they were flesh-and-blood people.

I was lucky, though. By arranging my work commitments, I made sure I had plenty of time with Jay, and I'm grateful for that. I got to watch him grow up, to share in all his moments of joy, and to be there for him in life's tougher moments. In a way, I was being a dad to myself - the dad I used to dream about during the dark days when I was scared, lost, and no one came to help me. No one came to tell me it was going to be okay or to give me even the most basic hug.

Even now, I find any form of hugs or affection really difficult. It feels awkward and uneasy, but I'm trying to overcome it. We have to learn to fix what is broken.

As I said, it's strange how, as we get older, we reflect on our lives. We realise what was right, what was wrong, and where we could have done better. Having Jay made me realise just how wrong everything Mrs Nobody put us through really was. When I looked at Jay, the thought of him enduring even one hour of my early life filled me with rage. I look back with sorrow, mourning what was lost through all the abuse. Sometimes it's too painful to process. For the first few years of counselling, I couldn't get through a single session without crying most of the way through.

Just to clarify, though, I'm not crying for myself as an adult. I cry for that little boy who was terrified in the dark, not knowing what was coming next. I wish I could go back in time, take him out of the home, and tell him, "Everything's going to be okay. I've got you now - no need to worry." But, of course, that's impossible, and I live with the consequences of what happened all those years ago. With Jay, however, I could make things right. I could protect him, right the wrongs, and give him the kind of life I never had.

And I did just that. I protected him like a lion, as well as my family and close friends. We had regular family holidays and amazing Christmases - even though I can't stand Christmas. Pauline and I gave Jay the magic of Christmas anyway.

CHAPTER 17:

CRAZINESS AND SUPERHEROES

By my forties, I still refused to let anything slide if I felt someone was trying to intimidate me or put me down. My drive to accept no bullshit was too strong. If someone came at me, I gave them exactly what they were looking for.

One example that stands out was when I was with one of my black belts from Glasgow - a guy called Mikee, a really cool guy. We'd just finished training on a Saturday and were heading through to Falkirk to pick up Pauline and his girlfriend, who were childhood friends and had been visiting someone there. When we got to the house, there was this guy I didn't like - he was the boyfriend of Pauline's friend. He'd given me a hard time because he knew I taught martial arts. I used to smile and ignore him, as Pauline had asked me to, and she knew that if I gave her my word, I'd stick to it.

That day, the guy had a mate over, and they'd been drinking all day. They were giving Mikee a hard time, slagging him off.

This guy had told me plenty of times before that he thought he could take me in a fight.

I'd just smile and say, "Probably," and then ignored him.

Normally, the first time someone said something like that, I'd have challenged them to "see how that turns out," but I'd promised Pauline I wouldn't engage.

While we were sitting there, Mikee went to the toilet, and as he came back into the room, one of the guys sucker-punched him around the door. I immediately jumped up, went to the first guy - the one who'd mouthed off to me - and punched him multiple times in the head within seconds. The last punch sent him flying into a corner table, which broke under him. I turned to the second guy, the one who'd hit Mikee, and started punching him in the head too.

The first guy managed to get up behind me, grabbed a table leg from the broken table, and swung it as hard as he could into my head, just above my right eye. The impact opened a gash so deep you could almost see my skull. I turned to him and said, "I'm from the Highlands - you're going to have to kill me to beat me." Then I knocked him down again.

By now, the room was chaos - girls were screaming, but I wasn't bothered. It wasn't the first time I'd been hit with something, nor the first time I'd had blood streaming down my body. I didn't care. I just wanted to go to war until no one was left standing.

Eventually, the police arrived. They saw the hole in my head and wanted me to go to the hospital, but I couldn't have cared less. I told them what had happened, and they could see the broken table and the blood everywhere. The funny thing? The guy who said he could beat me in a fight went down in five seconds, and his mate resorted to using a weapon and still couldn't finish me. I even laughed in his face.

I went to the hospital for a head scan and stitches. The next day, the police interviewed me and told me they were happy that the other guys had started the fight and used a weapon. I told them I didn't want to press charges or go to court - I'd handle it myself. However, because of the severity of my injury, the case went forward anyway.

At the court case, one of the guys had told his older brother about me, and the brother started mouthing off in the reception area. I told him, "Let's go outside and sort it out after the court case." Later, as I left the court, their car passed by mine. Seeing it as a threat, I jumped out of the car immediately. This was caught on the court cameras, and the police came out. I didn't care. Like I said, if you try to intimidate or threaten me, I'd rather die than back down.

Luckily, the police knew the guy and his history of trouble, so they told me to leave it and go home, which I did. As I said, I'm used to violence, and I have no fear of anyone.

Around this time, I had a strong desire to give something back to the world. I'd been thinking about what I could do and initially considered volunteering at a dog centre since I've always loved dogs. But then I had an idea that truly appealed to me - something that combined the skills I'd developed through my two biggest passions in life: breakdancing and martial arts.

The idea was to dress up as a superhero, but I wanted to go all out. I wanted the best, most realistic costume possible - something so convincing that kids couldn't tell it wasn't the real deal. Then, I'd bring in the dynamic moves I'd learned over the years to make the performance ultra-real. The goal was to visit sick kids in hospitals or children in need and put on a show that would bring them joy.

I started researching superhero costumes, but I quickly realised how expensive this idea would be. Some of the ultra-realistic costumes, like Iron Man, were priced at around seven thousand pounds. I knew I'd have to find a way to raise the money to fund the costumes and cover the costs of hospital visits. That's when it hit me: I could fund the project by doing kids' parties. The income from the parties could be reinvested into buying new costumes and supporting the hospital visits.

I discussed the idea with Pauline, and she immediately jumped on board. She helped set everything up, creating a Facebook page and ordering the first batch of suits. And with that, our company - Central Superheroes Parties and Events - was born.

I reached out to a few friends I'd taught breakdancing and martial arts to see if they wanted to be involved. Once we got our first batch of costumes, we secured our first booking. This was a huge relief, as we had gone into a few thousand pounds of debt to buy the gear. But we'd made a start.

On our first job, both the kids and the adults were blown away - not just by how lifelike the costumes were, but by the performances too. The "heroes" were doing jump kicks, backflips, and breakdancing across the floor. Before we knew it, our Facebook page started gaining loads of followers, and we were receiving hundreds of emails every day.

Once we were more established, we reached out to Glasgow Sick Kids Hospital, explaining what we did and asking if we could come in to do a show and visit the children. They agreed, and our first visit was incredibly emotional. Most of the team admitted to crying afterward. It was deeply humbling to see what the families were going through - their bravery left a lasting mark on me. But at the same time, we were thrilled to see the joy we were able to bring. It felt like such an honour to do what we did for those families.

Over the years, we've visited the hospital many times and have also performed for children in end-of-life care. When we see stories in the papers about families going through such heartbreaking situations, we reach out to offer our services free of charge. Our goal is to bring even a small moment of joy during their darkest times.

I can't tell you how many times I've had tears streaming down my face while inside my costume. Luckily, I perform as Bumblebee, so I do body popping and robotics, and my face is completely covered. It's just as well, as these moments are so emotional. The guys on the team are absolutely brilliant - they give up their spare time to join visits and always give 100%. Performing in those costumes is no easy task - they're incredibly hot and sweaty, especially in hospitals, which are warm to begin with. But it's all beyond worth it. It's one of the most rewarding things I've ever done.

We've also done a lot of charity shows and feel blessed to be able to give back. This year, Central Superheroes won *Scottish Business of the Year*, which completely blew us away. It was such a proud moment and proof that hard work really does pay off. Pauline, the team, and I work incredibly hard to be the best we can possibly be.

We've performed at massive events in front of thousands of people, turned on the Christmas lights for cities, and entertained for some of the biggest companies in Scotland. But above all else, we've brought joy to thousands of children, including so many who have endured the toughest challenges life can throw at them.

Now, we have the best quality suits available, and for the kids, it's pure magic. They truly believe their favourite hero has come to see them. We make each child the star of the show, and for those moments, nothing else matters. It's good to give back.

This time in my life was all about the grind. In my forties, I was still performing and breakdancing. During the week, I would teach private lessons during the day and go into schools to teach anti-bullying sessions. I focused on teaching kids to be kind and to have the confidence to be whoever they wanted to be in life, as long as they were kind. In the evenings, I taught martial arts classes, and on weekends, I was busy with superhero shows - Saturday and Sunday, every single week. We had no spare time, and that came at a cost.

Because of the nature of kids' parties, we said we would never miss one or let a child down. That commitment meant we missed out on a lot of things - weekends away with friends, weddings, and get-togethers - anything that happened on a weekend was out of the question. But our reputation became built on two things: having the best costumes and performers and never, ever cancelling a party. In ten years, we've never broken that promise.

There was one time a lady messaged Pauline at the last minute, desperate for a party for her child. Pauline explained we were fully booked, and the lady wrote back offering to pay an extra thousand pounds on top of the party price if we would cancel someone else's booking. I replied to her myself, saying, "I would never be able to look myself in the mirror if I caused a child's party to be cancelled just for money." I know exactly what disappointment feels like and I never want to be responsible for that hence why we have never let a kid down ever that's really important to me Above all else, we made sure to be people of our word. All our performers know the golden rule: we never miss a party.

I've worked through illness - even with a broken toe - but I still showed up, put on the suit, and got the job done.

As I get older, I find myself reflecting on the path my life could have taken. For whatever reason - and I believe it's down to the guidance of the kind people I've met along the way - I've always had a sense of wanting to do the right thing. Give it your best, bring a little joy, and your mission is complete.

Even as a young child, I understood the power of those amazing moments of kindness. They became deeply ingrained in me. The responsibility of passing that kindness on to others quietens my soul and brings me inner peace.

Now, at fifty-five, I still put on my superhero costume. I sweat, I perform, and it brings me so much joy to see the happiness it creates. I love speaking to parents afterwards when they say, "Wow, that was incredible - you made my child's birthday." There's no feeling like it.

And you know that when that child grows up, they'll remember the day our team came to their party and brought the magic. You can't ask for a better reward than knowing you've made a difference - no matter how small. Golden memories last a lifetime.

But then again, so do the painful ones.

That's why I made a vow: to try my hardest never to be the one creating the sad memories - only the good. And I'm happy with that. Our team has brought thousands of amazing memories into the world.

Central Superhero parties and events bringing joy to the kids at a show

Bringing joy to the Glasgow Sick Kids hospital

CHAPTER 18:

WHAT IS AFTER DEATH?

Me and death have had a funny connection over the years. I've spent so many years trying to understand death, and what it means to be alive and human. I've studied Zen Buddhism for the last twenty years, and I've explored loads of esoteric subjects, trying to understand what my purpose was, and why I had to have the tough journey I've had. And yeah, there are people in life who get dealt way tougher cards than I did, but I still needed to believe there was a reason behind it all.

I've studied everything from quantum science to UFOs to NDEs - or near-death experiences. And over the years, plenty of bizarre and unexplainable things have happened to me and my family. I honestly believe the world and the universe are not what we think they are. It's way more bizarre than we can even imagine.

Now, a few years ago, when Jay was about three years old and we lived in our first flat, Pauline had downloaded a sleep app on her iPhone to record any noises during the night. One night, Jay stirred and climbed into our bed between us. The next morning, Pauline was all excited to

181

check the recording - she thought she might've been sleep-talking. But what she heard shook her to the core.

At first, you hear Pauline sleep-talking. She says, "I can hear you."

Then, clear as day, there's a reply - from a strange voice that sounds like an old, angry Glaswegian man. He makes a sort of loud, smirking grunt. Now, on its own, that would've been weird but maybe still explicable. But what happened next, I still can't explain.

On the recording, you hear Jay climbing into our bed. Silence for a few minutes. Then Jay says, "If you touch that again, I would die."

The same Glaswegian voice responds, clear as anything, saying, "Get tae fuck."

My first thought was - has someone broken into the flat in the middle of the night? But we checked everything - doors, windows, all locked. Nothing out of place.

We played the recording to our friends, and every one of them was totally freaked out. No TV on. No sounds in the flat. It was the middle of the night. Jay was clearly responding to something, and so was Pauline. We couldn't explain it.

That flat was full of strange goings-on. Our friends who stayed over experienced things too - footsteps in the hallway, walking straight towards them, even when no one was there. Things flying off shelves that had sat untouched for years.

One night, Pauline and I were in bed. She was watching telly, and I was reading. We suddenly heard two loud knocks on the wooden headboard - right between us. I jumped up, heart racing. It was that clear. There was no explanation for it. None. That wasn't a one-off either. It happened more times than I can count.

Our three closest pals at the time - folk who stayed over often - they all had similar experiences in that flat. It got to the point where it was just part of our life there.

Pauline put the recording on Bebo - this was before Facebook - and loads of people commented, saying it was freaky. Then one guy messaged us. He said, "That voice sounds identical to my grandad." Then it turned out that his grandad used to live in our flat.

We were stunned. I mean, what are the chances?

Even in the house we live in now, odd things have happened. Sometimes with three or more people there to witness it. It's made me believe, even more strongly, that there's way more to this world than we understand.

I tried to understand our purpose, so I went deeper into researching NDEs - near-death experiences. I've listened to over a hundred of them online, and what blew me away was how similar they all are.

Typically, someone dies - an accident or a medical emergency - and suddenly they feel themselves out of their body. They might be floating near the ceiling or standing beside their body, watching. Then they feel themselves being pulled upwards, either through a tunnel at high speed or into this vast, dark void. And even in the darkness, they feel complete bliss.

Eventually, they see a light - sometimes a beautiful place filled with colours they've never seen before. Some see long-lost relatives. Then they meet a being of pure love, and often they go through something called a life review - re-living all the good and bad things they did, but from the perspective of the people they affected. They feel everything. The hurt, the joy, all of it. Like it's a kind of lesson.

These experiences are the same across people of all religions and ethnicities. Many happen when the brain has zero activity - clinically dead - yet the person is having this vivid, powerful experience.

Often, a voice will tell them, "It's not your time. You have to go back." And almost always, they're told, "Everything is as it should be." Then they're back in their body, disappointed they had to leave that beautiful place.

Over the last twenty years, I've meditated daily. And based on everything I've learned, I honestly believe we are not our body. The body is just a vessel - just a receiver. For want of a better word, we're souls, and we're here to learn.

It's like a school - or maybe a university. Think about it: if you come from a place of pure perfection, where you know all knowledge and everything is blissful, then what's the point? You'd never grow. Growth only comes from experience.

I believe we come here for a different kind of knowledge - spiritual growth.

Here's the crazy part: I think the harder the life you have here, the more growth and learning you achieve - and the more you can share when you go back to the other side.

What if all the film stars, the mega-beautiful people with all the money, were actually the lower souls who came here for the easy lesson?

And what if all the down-and-outs - the folk with addictions, the ones who battled and struggled through really hard lives - were actually the highest-level souls? The ones who took on lessons few could endure.

Wouldn't that be something? The ones we think are amazing are actually the weakest souls, and the ones society looks down on are the strongest.

Read that again - and take it in.

Studying NDEs has brought me a deep sense of peace about life and death. I don't believe in death now - not really. I believe it's just a return to where we came from, to what we really are. Souls in the shape of humans. Here for the lesson.

And if, like NDEs suggest, we choose our life experience before we come here - well, when I get back to the other side, I'm having a serious word with myself!

Next time, I'm coming back as a pop star or something easy - I've done enough of the tough stuff in this life. I've learned more about the nature of people than I ever wanted to.

When we lose someone we love, it teaches us what really matters. It's not money. Not possessions. None of that means anything at the end. What we want is our loved ones by our side. The things we own will become someone else's clutter eventually.

So, while we're here, we need to treasure the real gift of life: the love we share with those who care about us.

For me, losing people I love has reminded me of that truth again and again. Love is the universal currency - but most people don't realise that until it's too late.

Over the years, I've come to believe that life is one big lesson, and we're always learning. I reckon the final lesson comes in our last moments. That's when we finally get it - that the true meaning of everything is unconditional love.

That's where my head's at these days.

I look back at the lessons of my life - all the pain, the fear, the hurt - and I try to get the message, to grow from it. To find peace in who I am.

It's not easy. I'm not there yet. But something's shifting. Slowly, I'm understanding the lesson.

Like I said, I've lost my fear of death. I explain it like this:

Imagine a TV showing EastEnders. Now take a hammer and smash the telly. The TV is gone - but EastEnders still exists. The signal's still there. You've just broken the receiver.

That's what I think the body is. A receiver or antenna for your soul, which comes from somewhere else.

So, when your body dies, your soul doesn't - it lives on. Eternal.

It's hard to explain, but I hope you understand what I mean. I'm not great at getting the thoughts in my head out in the right way - and even worse at trying to write them down.

By now my martial arts classes were thriving, and in Edinburgh, we decided it was time to expand and establish our own full - time martial arts studio. A permanent base for the students felt like the next logical step, but it wasn't going to be easy - or cheap. After all, it was Edinburgh, where everything comes with a high price tag.

After much searching, we found an industrial unit down in Leith. It was ideal for our needs, and although the costs would be tight, we could just about manage the payments. The next challenge was acquiring the property and securing the necessary permissions. The unit required a change of use planning from light industrial to leisure, which turned out to be a process far more complicated than we'd anticipated. We had to submit planning applications to the council, covering everything from fire regulations to parking and the potential impact on the local area.

We had negotiated a three - month rent - free period with the landlord to help us get established and build up our presence in the area. We knew that moving to other side of the city would mean losing some students, but we hoped to gain new ones. In the meantime, we were still paying rent on the building we'd been using before the studio opened.

We thought it would take a month or two to get everything approved, allowing us to get in and start the necessary work. But it didn't go as planned. The council dragged its heels, turning one month into two, then four, and finally six. By the time the three - month free period ended, we still didn't have approval, and we had started paying rent on a building we couldn't even use.

Desperate to move forward, we contacted local MPs and enlisted their support, explaining how beneficial a family martial arts studio would be for the area. It wasn't just about fitness or self - defence - it was about bringing families together and creating a positive community hub.

Eventually, with their backing, we managed to get the planning approved.

It was one of the most stressful times of my life. I was trying to push everything through while running two martial arts schools, managing personal training clients, teaching breakdancing, and setting up the superhero shows. There simply weren't enough hours in the day. Pauline and I were both mentally and physically shattered, but in the end, we made it. My dream had come true: my own martial arts gym in Edinburgh.

When we finally opened, the real grind began. Almost as soon as we moved in, the bills started piling up. On top of the rent, there was building insurance, water rates, heating, electricity - you name it. The financial pressure was immense, so we worked even harder to cover the costs.

Living in Falkirk added another challenge. It took about an hour to get to the studio in good traffic, which meant even more time out of our already packed days. But needs must, and my attitude has been not to make excuses, just get on with it. In fact, I had the words *No Excuses* painted on one of the studio walls as a constant reminder to myself and my students.

I've always believed that a strong work ethic is the foundation for achieving great things in life. I've never subscribed to the mindset of blaming my difficult childhood for my circumstances. Instead, I used my childhood as fuel to drive my passion for building a better life. Excuses, in my view, are for others - not for me.

The strange thing I've found, though, is that when you're driven and passionate about being the best version of yourself - both physically and in your working life - jealousy often rears its ugly head. Some people hate to see others succeed, and their jealousy can turn into resentment. It's ironic because I started with absolutely nothing. Everything I've achieved, I've earned the hard way. I've never taken a shortcut or relied on handouts.

But the green - eyed monster is a weakness for others, not for me. Over the years, I've learned that if you focus on self - improvement and building a better life for your family, you need to develop a thick skin. As soon as you start achieving things, that's when the backstabbing and bitching begin.

I used to think, *if they only knew what it took to get here, they'd see things differently.* The adage "If you walk a mile in my shoes" rings true. I knew that most of my haters wouldn't have lasted an hour in my early life, let alone a day. But, as my instructor reminded me, *you must have a thick skin. Haters do nothing but hate - that's just what they do.*

To be honest, I couldn't give a toss about people disliking me - I've dealt with it all my life, even when I had nothing. The funny thing is, as soon as you start making progress or achieving something in life, people seem to dislike you even more. But life isn't a popularity contest, and you'll never be liked by everyone. I've learned that it's not about being liked by everyone - it's about being liked by the *right* ones. The ones who aren't intimidated by your success or growth.

My approach to life has been simple: do no harm but take no shit. Of course, life isn't that straightforward, but I try my best to be a good person. We're all human, though - we stumble and fall. The key is not to stay down. You pick yourself up, dust yourself off, and get back into the world.

What I've discovered is that in the process of trying to make a difference in the world, I've also been able to make a living doing the things I love. It's funny how the universe works. It doesn't give you what you *want* - it gives you what you *need*. And in turn, it gives you growth and fulfilment.

The one thing I can't stand in a person is bitching behind someone's back. To me, it's the lowest form of self - expression. Unfortunately, I've found that the moment you start achieving anything in life, that's when the backbiting and gossip start. I've always been a positive, motivational person, and I've tried to help others. But over time, I realised you can't change everyone's opinions, and so I stopped caring. My attitude became: *Let them.* The people who moan, gossip, and backstab are usually the ones who lack the discipline to help themselves. Instead, they project their frustrations onto those they envy.

I have regularly said, "It's none of my business what others think of me." And honestly, if those people had walked a mile in my shoes, they wouldn't have lasted an hour in my early life, let alone a day.

I never made excuses about my hard start in life. Instead, I used it as fuel to create a life less ordinary. Over the years of teaching martial arts and running anti - bullying workshops in schools, I've had a positive impact on thousands of people. That's more than enough for me.

I'd also started doing some life coaching through my personal training clients and was once invited to run a life coaching workshop for an oil company. I brought a few of my black belts with me and shared some of the lessons I'd learned over the years. It was fascinating to me - many of these guys earned more in a month than most people see in a year, but as I pointed out to them while we all sat on the floor in the hall, some things are far more valuable than money.

I told them to imagine we all spoke different languages, and no one understood the others. If you tried to say, "I earn this much" or "I'm the head of this company," it wouldn't mean anything. But if I ran up a wall, did a back somersault, and broke a board in mid - air, everyone would clap. Physicality is a universal language - it doesn't matter where you're from, everyone can appreciate the skill and hard work it takes to achieve something like that.

That's how I've looked at the world. I've never been impressed by money or material possessions. I earn enough to pay my bills and put a roof over my family's head, but as Pauline will tell you, I never ask for money for anything. My motivation comes from moving forward in life, bringing positivity into the world, and helping people achieve things they never thought possible.

I often think about what the world could be if we all did one small act of kindness every day. Nothing huge - just one small thing. With billions of people on the planet, imagine how much better things could be. I know it makes me sound like an old hippie, but I truly believe in the power of one: one person, one act, one step in the right direction.

Our greatest legacy is the difference we make in the lives of others, no matter how small. I've seen people transform not only their own lives but their entire families' lives through exercise and martial arts. It amazes me how the universe has given us the greatest gift of all: the power to change our lives in an instant. Like the old proverb says, "A journey of a thousand miles begins with a single step." I always add that the step must be in the *right* direction, and it's up to us to take it.

Over the years, I've worked with kids who've come from nothing. Through sheer will and determination, they've carved out great lives for themselves and their families. They've done it the right way - through hard work and perseverance. That's the power within all of us. You just have to put in the work, never quit, and keep grinding. The biggest room in the world is the room for self - improvement.

Although life was incredibly busy and full of hard work, it was wonderful to see everything heading in the right direction. Family holidays with Jay were amazing. I got to do so many things with him that I never got to experience as a child. Growing up in care, we didn't really go on holidays because of budgets and limitations, but I made sure Jay had the best experiences. We went to Disney, travelled abroad, and loved our trips to Haven Holidays. Jay absolutely adored it, and we made magical memories during those times.

In my mind, I was determined to give Jay everything I never had. Part of me hoped that by giving him such a happy and secure childhood, it might fix some of my inner demons. But life isn't that simple. Some things can't be fixed, no matter what you do. Instead, you must find ways to cope and navigate through life with the baggage you carry.

What I found particularly hard was looking at Jay and seeing how happy, loved, and secure he was. While it filled me with love for him, it also broke my heart. It reminded me of myself at his age - full of fears and insecurities. I love my son more than anything in this world, but for myself, I harboured nothing but self - hatred. It's strange how those feelings were triggered. Don't get me wrong - I cherished every second I spent with Jay. He was the reason I lived. But his happiness shone a spotlight on my past and made me realise how much I would have given for a normal, loving childhood. Nothing fancy, just normal.

Later, my counsellor explained that this was a common experience, but it didn't make it any easier. Although things were going great on the surface - work was successful, and life looked positive - I was struggling with the thoughts in my head. My CPTSD was starting to win the battle, and the constant urge to self-destruct was always there, lurking.

I concluded that if I didn't get help, things wouldn't end well. A few times, when my mental health hit rock bottom, I went to my GP completely broken. There were moments when I'd break down in tears during our conversations, especially when he asked about my life or my past.

I'd been told more than once that I had CPTSD, but my brain dismissed it. Somehow, I saw it as something shameful or as a weakness - something I was too mentally strong to have. Growing up in Scotland in the 70s, we were told to just "get on with it." Crying was out of the question. PTSD wasn't something I could entertain. Instead, I threw myself into more training, which helped to balance my mind a little. But it was only a temporary fix - a small plaster on a massive wound.

I never told anyone how low I felt, not even Pauline. To me, admitting that was a weakness, and I didn't allow myself to appear weak.

At the time, I was completely focused on being a good dad to Jay and providing for my family. That drive to give him the best possible life pushed me to work incredibly hard, even with the added stress of parenting and paying the bills. I was determined that Jay would never face the struggles I had endured. As a parent, I knew I couldn't overprotect him - life would inevitably present its own hardships, which he'd need to grow and survive - but I wanted to make his journey as smooth as I could.

My forties were a strange time. I knew something wasn't right with my thought processes, and I could feel that my emotions were broken. I would wake up early in the morning, go downstairs by myself, and just cry for no apparent reason. It was a sadness that overwhelmed me completely, something I had no control over. It's hard to explain, but I started searching for answers, like I always did when I didn't understand something. I became obsessed with finding out what was wrong and began reading everything I could about CPTSD and Functional Neurological Disorder (FND).

Living with both has been incredibly tough. It affects every second of your day and every action you take. It also affects everyone you interact with because your brain constantly calculates every possible scenario and outcome, always searching for threats. From the moment I first noticed something was wrong to the point of finally being diagnosed, it was about a twelve - year journey.

I think, as I slowed down physically, my past started to catch up with me. When I was younger, I was moving too fast - constantly striving for success in martial arts, breakdancing, and business. By my forties, I had reached a stable point where everything came together. My businesses were thriving, I had a nice house, and we had a nice car. Pauline and I had worked incredibly hard for it, sacrificing nearly every weekend for the past ten years and missing out on countless social events. As I said Our hard work was recognised when our business was crowned the best in Scotland at the Scottish Business Awards.

You'd think that achieving all this would calm the demons in my mind, but it didn't. I realised that success couldn't fix the deeper issues I was grappling with.

CHAPTER 19:

STRUGGLES

While things were going really well externally throughout my forties, I was trying to cope with the increasing symptoms of FND. It was challenging in ways I could never have anticipated. Sometimes, in the middle of a conversation, I'd forget what I was saying, and no matter how hard I tried to remember, the thought would just slip further away. When it got particularly bad, I'd slur my words or struggle to speak at all. It usually happened after long days of teaching under fluorescent lights. I'd feel shaky, sick, and as though I'd drunk six pints of beer.

What I found hardest was explaining this to people. I've prided myself on my sharp mind, especially when it comes to recalling thousands of Kuk Sool techniques in an instant. But during an FND attack, I struggled to recall even simple things, like a friend's name. Thankfully, it didn't last long, and once I was under normal lighting, the symptoms would start to subside. Even so, it was a humbling and frustrating experience.

As we get older, we tend to look back on life with the wisdom of experience, gaining a deeper understanding of events that shaped us. In my early forties, being a dad to Jay and having a normal, loving family life brought the past into sharp focus. The injustice of it all weighed heavily on my soul.

My battles with FND and PTSD became more pronounced and had a greater impact on my daily life. I couldn't escape the unfairness of it. This wasn't some random illness I just happened to develop - it was caused by the childhood trauma I endured. And now, decades later, I was left to make sense of it all, with nearly no help from the NHS. Even reaching the point of diagnosis had been an uphill battle.

I knew I needed help to face the demons in my head, but I wasn't sure who to turn to. My GP had been almost useless, dismissing my symptoms and offering little more than "try these tablets." I've never been one for medication, so that wasn't an option for me. Instead, I did what I'd always done I moved faster, trained harder, and worked longer. I tried to outrun the thoughts in my head, believing that if I stayed busy enough, I wouldn't have to confront the darkness.

By this point, all my businesses were doing well. Pauline and I had built a good standard of living for ourselves, and the years passed as we worked hard to provide Jay with a stable, loving home. We took family holidays and created special memories so Jay would have the best start in life.

Three times a week, I'd travel to my full - time martial arts gym in Edinburgh, and the rest of the week, I taught classes in Falkirk. On weekends, we ran superhero parties for kids. Life was full - on, with barely half a day off, but the hard work paid off.

We continued our charity work, visiting sick kids in Glasgow and CHAS House for children with terminal cancer. I firmly believe that if you can bring a moment of joy to someone in their darkest times, you should do it. Pauline shared this belief, and we were ready to help anyone in need.

On the surface, everything was going great. But inside, I was fighting a relentless battle with the thoughts in my head. I had never truly processed my past, and honestly, I didn't even know where to begin. There were dark memories I'd never shared with another living soul - not my partner, not my family, not my best friend. I didn't even allow myself to think about them. It was a no - go subject, but I knew it was eating away at me.

The more I learned about FND and PTSD, the more I realised how much of it stemmed from Mrs Nobody and the abuse she inflicted on me. While there were others who had physically hurt me in the home, the real, lasting damage came from her - mentally and physically. Unless you've lived through it, no words can truly explain the depth of the harm. It changes how your brain forms, and I firmly believe no amount of counselling can ever undo that damage. The scars are permanent.

One of the most important people in my life - Christine Gray

The last picture I got of Christine. She was like a mum to me.

CHAPTER 20:

A PAINFUL LOSS

Over the years, I kept in close contact with Christine Gray and visited her every time I was home. She was my mum when my mum had passed, and we were incredibly close. She had my back, gave me unconditional support, and for that, I feel truly blessed.

During my forties, I lost several good friends, some to natural causes and others to suicide. One of those friends, Yini, passed away, and it hit me hard. He was a couple of years younger than me, but we just clicked, and his death knocked me for six. Another old pal, Kenny - known to everyone as Cooter - died of cancer. I travelled up to see him a couple of times when he was ill, and it was brutal to witness.

It was a strange time, marked by a lot of loss. One of my black belts from back in Thurso took his own life, and two of my students passed away. One of them was in a car accident, and the day that was meant to be his wedding was changed to his funeral. I had to present his partner with an honorary black belt at the service, and it was one of the hardest things I've ever had to do. Another former student, a girl I used to teach martial arts and personal train, died suddenly of a heart attack at her workplace.

It felt like one loss after another, and it knocked me sideways. I've never been good with death and loss, especially when it's people I'm close to. The weight of it all made my mental health spiral. That's the thing with CPTSD - it strips you of the ability to regulate your emotions, and the looping thoughts of loss can completely overwhelm you.

I've had this strange ability to feel others' pain as if it were my own, which only makes it harder. One time I was on the phone with Ali, when I was really struggling with my mental health. I told her, "My problem is that I care too much. It's my greatest weakness."

She corrected me. She said, "No, you've got that wrong. That's your greatest strength. You wear your heart on your sleeve, and you should never change that." She had the best advice for me and knew exactly what to say, no matter the situation.

Until that point, I had never attended a funeral, but in the space of a couple of years, I found myself at four. I was once at the funeral of the girl I used to personal train and teach martial arts to. During the eulogy, they mentioned the impact I had on her life. It completely caught me off guard and broke me emotionally. It was a powerful reminder that, as we walk through life, we leave footprints in others' lives - often without even realising it. I'm grateful to have been a positive influence in her life, but the loss was still devastating.

What I've found hardest over the years is the change that comes with losing people. Things that used to feel so solid and unshakable to me in my youth started to disappear.

One of the biggest losses of my life was still to come, and it shattered me to the very core. As I mentioned, I visited Christine every time I was home, and we stayed incredibly close. I last saw her at her retirement event, where I gave a speech about the enormous impact she'd had on my life. I spoke about how she had supported me after I came out of care, how she had been one in a million, and how much I credited her and her family for shaping the person I became. Christine taught me how to be kind and caring, and so much of who I am today is because of her love and guidance.

Around Christmas one year, I tried to get in touch with her when I was home, but I couldn't reach her. I'd heard she had been in hospital but was getting answers and on the mend. Then, one weekend, just as I was getting ready for a superhero party, a message popped up on my phone from Christine's sister, Bettine. The message read: I'm sorry to tell you, Christine has passed away.

I fell off my seat. The news was so unexpected that I let out a yell of pure pain. Pauline came running to see what had happened. It's still, to this day, one of the most painful moments of my life. What made it worse was that I still had to perform at a kids' party that day - and I wasn't going to let a child down. Thankfully, still playing Bumblebee, my face was hidden behind a mask. It was the hardest performance of my life. Inside, I was falling apart.

For weeks after her death, I cried every day. The pain was soul - crushing. I travelled to Thurso for Christine's funeral, but I can't remember any of it - it was a complete blur. Christine's good friend, Mags, sat next to me and helped me through it, but the grief was overwhelming. I never imagined life without her, and the pain consumed me.

At night, Pauline would wake up to find me sitting on the stairs, sobbing. I couldn't cope with the loss. My eyes became raw and painful from crying so much. At my absolute lowest point, something strange happened - something I still can't fully explain.

I was in my room, crying, when the TV suddenly crackled with static, the fuzzy dots you see when it's not tuned in. Then, clear as day, I heard Christine's voice. She said, "Now come on, that's enough," in a firm but loving way. I jumped up, my heart racing. It was exactly what she would have said to me.

To this day, I don't know if it was a lucid dream or if I was awake, but to me, it felt entirely real. From that moment onward, I started to cope a little better, day by day. Even in death, Christine somehow managed to rescue me again.

It took me years to be able to mention her name without breaking down. That's the hard part of FND and CPTSD - they heighten and completely derail your ability to regulate emotions. There's no control, none at all. You can burst out crying in the middle of a meeting if something triggers you, and it's deeply embarrassing at times.

Christine's passing left a hole in my life that will never be filled, but I carry her lessons with me every day. She taught me how to be kind, caring, and strong. I'll never forget her, and I am grateful for the love she gave me.

Every time I go back home to Thurso, I visit Christine's grave. I take her fresh flowers and talk to her about everything happening in my life. I tell her how much I miss her and how I look forward to seeing her again when it's my time to go to the other side. She was the mum I never had, and I miss her greatly.

Over time, I worked on coming to terms with my new reality after being diagnosed. Of course, I had known something was wrong, but it's hard to admit you have a problem. For men, in particular, mental health is often a taboo subject. Growing up in the Highlands in the seventies, it was drilled into us that men don't cry and that you need to "man up" when faced with life's problems. I now realise what utter bullshit that is. It took more strength than anything else in my life to admit I had problems and that I needed help.

I knew if I didn't address my mental health, the outcome would not be good. To be clear, the trauma that led to this wasn't my fault. There's a version of me that never went through the things I did, a version of me that didn't spend decades keeping those experiences bottled up. I reached out countless times to my GPs for help, but I got nothing in return. One doctor even told me to "pull myself together." I realised I needed to look elsewhere and find help from people who understood what I was going through.

My sister, Kath, had mentioned a group called Future Pathways that she had spoken to. It took me about a year to work up the courage to contact them. I finally called and spoke to a lady who took some details and sent me a form to fill out. Once I sent it back, I was told there was a fairly long waiting list to be assigned a caseworker. For me, it took about a year.

By the time I had my first appointment, my mental health was in a terrible state. Here's the thing about mental health issues - they can deceive you. Your brain convinces you that you're worthless, and in my case, I felt like I had ruined the lives of everyone I'd ever met. I could only see my mistakes, the times I had fallen short as a man, a father, and a partner. The worst part is how something small and insignificant to others can become enormous to you. You dwell on your perceived failings, completely blind to your successes.

CPTSD is insidious like that. It warps the way you see yourself and makes you believe everyone else sees you the same way.

After a rough year battling my inner demons, I had my first meeting with a counsellor. She asked where I would feel most comfortable for the session, and I chose my house. When the day arrived, I was so nervous that my heart was pounding out of my chest. I'm a very private person, especially about my past, and the thought of speaking to a stranger about my darkest secrets terrified me.

But by then, I knew the alternative was far worse. I had started spiralling into suicidal thoughts - dark, relentless thoughts. Now, I need to be clear: I would never act on those thoughts. I love my family far too much to put them through that pain. But I was completely worn out by life. I was done. Everything felt too hard. I had fought every single day of my life to get ahead, and it felt like that fight had drained me completely.

When you've been grinding since birth and have faced things most people can't imagine, it wears you down. That special energy you once had eventually runs out, leaving you empty, broken, and feeling worthless. Your own thoughts become your worst enemy, and you yearn for an escape - not from life, but from the endless noise in your head. I'd often wonder who that voice in my head was, the one saying, "It's been too hard. You've endured too much." I don't know who they were, but they were relentless and unceasing.

Our full time martial arts studio in Leith, Edinburgh
Sadly it had to close due to Covid

CHAPTER 21:

CONFRONTING THE DARKNESS

I'd always believed I was mentally tough - one of the toughest. And I was. But even the strongest mountain can erode under a constant drip of water. That's what mental health issues do: they slowly eat away at who you are, until one day, you wake up and feel like it's all too much. You just want peace from the demons in your head.

That's where I was when my counsellor, Nicola, arrived. I was like a cat on a hot tin roof. My heart was pounding, and I wanted to be anywhere but there. Pauline could see my anxiety and reassured me that I was doing the right thing. She told me she was there for me 100%.

Nicola introduced herself, and we went into the living room. Pauline asked if I wanted her to stay, but I said no. There were things in my past - like the sexual abuse - that I hadn't even told her. I didn't want her to know, and I certainly didn't want to verbalise it. I could barely think about it myself, let alone speak it out loud to anyone else.

I didn't know what to expect from the session, but Nicola put me at ease. She was kind and told me that everything I said was up to me - there would be no judgment, only full support and belief. That was massive for me. For years, my past had been a taboo subject, something I couldn't talk about at any cost.

When I finally started talking, the floodgates opened. I think I cried more that day than I ever have in my life. It was incredibly hard to say some of the things that had been weighing so heavily on my soul. But admitting I needed help was the biggest step I'd ever taken.

For my entire life, I had built myself into this impenetrable machine, immune to anything life could throw at me. Admitting that I was broken deep down felt like a total failure. It felt like I had betrayed the deal I'd made with myself to never let the past get the better of me. But I've since realised that there's no healing without acknowledging that something is broken in the first place.

Now, I don't like to say, "something is wrong," even though I've used those words here for the sake of clarity. Mental health isn't about being "wrong." It's simply the state we find ourselves in as a response to the things we've experienced.

After four years of counselling, I've learned that being open and honest about mental health is the truest form of bravery. Admitting you need help isn't a weakness - it's a strength. Saying, "It's okay not to be okay," and reaching out for love and support when you need it takes incredible courage.

The stigma of silence was slapped into us from a young age, but real strength lies in breaking that silence. I didn't feel that way during my first session - it was beyond painful and went against everything I thought I was. I felt exposed and broken. But I realised that was the CPTSD trying to control my thoughts yet again.

That day, I drew a line in the sand. I was done with the guilt, the shame, and the broken feeling. I was done waking up every morning at five, going downstairs alone, and crying uncontrollably from the depths of my soul. That wasn't living - it was robbing me of my joy and stopping me from seeing a future.

After my first session with Nicola, she asked what I had planned for the rest of the day and advised me to rest and relax, as I would feel drained. She wasn't wrong. I apologised for being such a teary wreck, but she reassured me that it was completely normal and that she was proud of me for opening up. Her support was incredible, and she explained that talking about my past was the path to healing, even if I couldn't see it at the time. She told me that as the months went on, it would become easier to talk about - even the abuse - and eventually, I'd be able to speak about it without being in tears. I honestly didn't believe that was possible.

After she left, I felt like I'd been hit by a truck. For three hours, I had been emotionally broken, and the aftermath left me with a splitting headache. I was wracked with guilt for talking about a dark secret that I had convinced myself should never be spoken of. Pauline gave me a big hug and told me she was proud of me, which meant the world. Nicola scheduled another appointment for a couple of weeks later and told me I could call her if I needed anything in the meantime.

A few days after our session, Nicola sent me a weighted blanket to help me sleep, along with an aromatherapy diffuser to use during my breathing exercises. She had already started working on a plan for my recovery. She also sent me a book called *The Body Keeps the Score*, which is brilliant and something I'd recommend to anyone trying to understand trauma.

It's only now that I realise burying your head in the sand doesn't help - it only makes things worse. That's exactly where CPTSD tries to take you: into despair and denial. The greatest tool we have is talking about it. Nicola also contacted mental health services to get me an official diagnosis, but the waiting list to see a psychiatrist was about a year. In the meantime, we scheduled regular face - to - face and telephone meetings.

To say this was the hardest time of my life would be an understatement. I had never been one to open up about my life to anyone. Whenever someone asked me where I was from or about my family, I would give the shortest answer possible and avoid elaborating. In the Highlands, it's common for people to ask who your mum or dad is as a way to place you. I would say, "My mum and dad are dead." That would inevitably lead to them saying, "Oh, I'm sorry to hear that," or "How did they die?" I'd simply reply, "They died when I was a kid," and end the conversation there.

Through counselling, I've changed a lot. Although it's been incredibly painful, I've come to realise that keeping secrets from friends and family slowly destroys you from the inside out. The constant overthinking and overanalysing wears you down until something has to give.

We're in a mental health crisis, and it's so important to understand that it's not weak to admit you're struggling. It's not weak to say you've had thoughts of ending it all. True strength lies in acknowledging what you perceive as weakness and reaching out for help.

For years, I felt so ashamed - ashamed of the abuse I'd suffered and ashamed to talk about it. I thought admitting to mental health issues meant I was mentally weak. But I now understand that the mental health problems I face were *done to me*. I was too young and too small to defend myself from what happened. That's why I've spent my life mastering combat sports and strengthening my mind, trying to protect myself from the ghosts of the past.

Future Pathways have been amazing, and Nicola understands me in ways I never thought possible. During our sessions, I would often get stuck in looping thoughts, repeatedly talking about the injustices I'd faced. Nicola would gently remind me why my brain was thinking that way, helping me make sense of the chaos.

Painful doesn't even begin to describe it. The dark memories I have are so tough to even think about, let alone verbalise. What bothers me most is the injustice of it all. Why me? I don't see myself as a victim, and it's not about saying, "Poor me." But imagine this: being put into care at the age of two, after your mother dies of cancer, and then being met with more trauma and abuse in a place that was meant to protect you. All this while living with the fear of having no parents and no normal family life.

I have to carry these thoughts with me every single day. Then the rage takes over - the rage at the injustice of it all. Why should I have CPTSD and FND because of the actions of staff who were supposed to care for me? Why should my life be broken?

Despite everything, I've fought every single day to be someone - to leave a positive mark on the world, to achieve things others thought impossible. Not to be better than anyone else, but to prove to myself that I am enough, that I matter, that I am worthwhile. And yes, even to believe that the world is a better place because I exist.

It's taken years of counselling to even begin to acknowledge that I can love myself. That I can be proud of surviving a life that was anything but ordinary. Not only did I survive, but I thrived. I created an extraordinary life filled with achievements and success, in spite of - and because of - my childhood.

You see, we can do remarkable things with the pain we endure. That's the life lesson, and it's why I believe I'm here. Through enduring, we gain a perspective that few people get to glimpse. Not all gifts are pleasant. Some are dark, painful, and hard. But those gifts shape us. They teach us kindness, compassion, and resilience.

As I write this, I realise it's impossible to fully convey the journey I've been on. Words can't adequately express the depth of the pain or the strength it's taken to keep going. But I'm being honest in sharing how my brain perceives the world after everything I've been through.

This book isn't about who will read my story - it's about taking the pain that's lived in my head for fifty years and putting it down onto paper.

Now, three years into seeking help, I'm finally able to talk about my past without breaking down. I can look back on my life with a new perspective and, dare I say, some understanding. Had these things not happened to me, I wouldn't be the person I am today. There's still a long way to go. Even as I write this, two years after my official diagnosis of CPTSD, I'm still waiting for mental health treatment to help me cope with it.

CPTSD dominates every thought and every action, all day, every day. But I'm learning to manage it. I'm learning that the most extraordinary growth comes from the deepest pain. And above all, I'm learning that it's okay not to be okay.

Every time I reflect on my experiences and the ongoing effects of my childhood, one thing stands out: the glaring injustice of how the Scottish Government and local councils have handled the aftermath of abuse suffered by those of us in their care. They should have a duty of care to the victims of abuse that occurred while we were under their responsibility. Instead, waiting two years for any mental health treatment for the CPTSD and FND caused by people they employed feels like being abused all over again.

I completely understand the immense strain on the NHS, particularly on mental health services, with their overwhelming waiting lists. But the Scottish Government should take responsibility for this historic abuse. They should fund private treatment for victims, ensuring we get the urgent help and support we so desperately need. After all, it was their system that failed us. Whatever safeguarding was meant to exist in the 1970s failed miserably, and we're left to carry the consequences.

CHAPTER 22:

REDRESS

The Scottish Government has now introduced something called *Redress*, which aims to provide financial compensation to victims of historic child abuse. There's a flat rate of ten thousand pounds, or you can present your case to a panel that reviews your records, medical evidence, and any eyewitness testimony to determine a compensation amount. These amounts start at twenty thousand pounds and can go up to forty, sixty, or a maximum of one hundred thousand pounds for the most severe cases.

But let's be honest - no amount of money can compensate for a lifetime of enduring the effects of abuse. If someone offered me five million pounds or the chance to erase everything I've gone through, I wouldn't hesitate. I'd say, "Keep your money. Just give me a normal life."

The journey to Redress was a difficult one. I hired a solicitor to explore my legal options, hoping for some form of justice. But I was told very quickly that, because Mrs Nobody had died, it would be nearly impossible to pursue a civil claim. Apparently, due to a law that makes it challenging to bring a case against someone who has passed away, it would be a non - starter - even if there were witnesses to the abuse.

It's breathtaking to think that the death of an abuser somehow erases the possibility of justice, even though the trauma they caused lives on. With no other options, I went down the Redress route.

The Redress process took about three years, and it was mentally and emotionally draining. You have to relive memories you'd rather forget, and worse still, you have to share them with your solicitor and the panel that reviews your case. The first time I called Emma, my solicitor, I was a mess. She was incredibly understanding, which was a lifeline for someone like me. With PTSD and FND, your emotions are so deregulated that you have zero control over them. It's exhausting and terrifying to talk about the most private, painful parts of your life, but Emma made it easier to take that step.

It's strange - I'm writing this book and sharing my story with all of you, yet talking about it with someone face - to - face feels completely different. For me, the purpose of this book is to take all the bad memories swimming around in my head and give them space to exist in a book instead. Once there, I can free myself of their unbidden burden and only revisit the thoughts if and when I choose to.

Writing this has been healing. It's given me the chance to face my life and reflect on why I've done the things I've done, as well as the profound hold CPTSD has on a person. Ten years ago, I had no concept of CPTSD. Like most people, I thought it was something soldiers developed from fighting in a war. But through counselling, I've learned that CPTSD can come from multi - layered trauma experienced over a long period of time. CPTSD, in particular, is incredibly debilitating.

The process of Redress involved gathering records from my time in the children's home, as well as finding witnesses who had experienced the same abuse at the hands of Mrs Nobody. That part, at least, was relatively straightforward. Anyone who was in the home during that time had their own memories and trauma caused by her.

I reached out to people I hadn't spoken to in over forty years to ask if they remembered what happened and whether they would provide a statement to my solicitor. Luckily, most of them agreed. Some, however, found it too painful to revisit those memories. While they talked to me and Pauline and confirmed everything I had said, they couldn't go on record. I completely understood and respected their decision. Still, I was fortunate to have many who were willing to come forward.

What I didn't expect was how many of them told me, "Donald, you're the first person I've ever spoken to about this." They were relieved to finally have someone to talk to, and in return, I helped them access support through Future Pathways or start their own Redress applications.

Where things got tougher was accessing my records. We enlisted Birth link to help, but they were shocked when they were initially told there were no records of me ever being in the children's home. It wasn't until they approached the legal deadline to produce the records and a call from my solicitor that the records "magically" appeared just before the deadline.

Even then, I knew something would be missing. I told my solicitor, "You won't find any records from the time I was in the home under Mrs Nobody." Sure enough, when they reviewed the files, they found a glaring gap. My records showed me entering the home at the age of two, but everything during the years Mrs Nobody was there was missing. Then, suddenly, the records restarted when I was about ten.

I have my own thoughts on why those years are missing.

It's surreal, gathering evidence to prove your own existence and the trauma you've endured. The entire process was mentally exhausting. You must face your darkest demons, and when you look into that darkness, it looks right back at you.

The injustice of it all is what weighs on me most. The abuse happened because of a system that was supposed to protect me. Safeguarding failed completely, and now the Scottish Government makes us relive these horrors to "prove" what we went through. Then, they offer compensation that doesn't come close to reflecting the lifetime of pain we've had to endure.

For me, it was never about the money - it was about justice, acknowledgment, and closure. What happened to me should never have happened to anyone. Yet the system that failed me in childhood continues to fail me as an adult. And still, the fight goes on.

CHAPTER 23:

BREAKING POINT

Life during this four - year period was some of the hardest I've ever experienced. We had just come out of the COVID - 19 pandemic, which hit my business hard - as it did for so many of us. In the first few weeks alone, over 60% of my students cancelled their payments for classes, and we had to cancel a huge number of bookings we had lined up. This, combined with the stress of the Redress process, sent my anxiety through the roof.

At the same time, my brother, Andrew, suffered a severe brain injury, leaving him hospitalised with a grim prognosis. When I travelled up to see him in Aberdeen, I was shocked by his condition. He couldn't recognise reality, speaking in confused and unsettling ways, saying the room was on fire or that he had been talking to dead people from our past. It was heartbreaking to see him like that, and it added another layer to the mental and emotional weight I was already carrying.

Meanwhile, we were dealing with the financial strain of keeping the martial arts studio in Edinburgh afloat. Edinburgh is an expensive city to run a business, and the government assistance provided during the pandemic barely scratched the surface. It didn't cover the rent on the studio, let alone the mortgage on our house, food, or other living expenses. Within a short period, all my savings were gone - used up on a building no one was even allowed to use.

The anxiety of it all was overwhelming, as there was no security and no clear end in sight to the pandemic. To adapt, we started teaching online classes to the students who stayed with us. It wasn't ideal, but it was a lifeline, and I am grateful to those who stuck with us. Still, the bills kept mounting, and we were sinking into debt.

On top of this, I was travelling back and forth to Aberdeen to visit Andrew, which made money even tighter. But my brother was my priority. The doctors wanted to move him into a care home because his cognitive ability was so poor. I knew that would be a serious problem, as Andrew had told me he would never go back into a care home environment - and I knew exactly why. Both of us had experienced the trauma of being in care as children, and the thought of him returning to that kind of setting was unbearable.

Luckily, I noticed small improvements in Andrew over the course of about six months. I had power of attorney for him, along with his wife, and during one of the team meetings with his doctors and support staff, I told them he would never go into care. I explained his history and our shared experiences in the children's home, and I was determined to honour his wishes.

Against all odds, Andrew made an incredible recovery. We had been told there was no hope, but he defied expectations and gradually returned to the brother I know and love. It was nothing short of amazing to see him back home and back to himself.

But while Andrew's story took a positive turn, my own mental health was spiralling. Between the financial strain of the pandemic, the stress of the Redress process, and the emotional toll of my brother's illness, I developed severe suicidal thoughts.

By 2022 and 2023, things had gotten really bad. I cried most days and thought about ways to end it all. I felt disgusted with myself for even thinking that way, but mental health doesn't play by the rules. It wears you down, and for me, the journey since birth had been so hard that I was completely worn out. Everything I had worked so hard to build seemed to be falling apart because of the pandemic.

There is a limit to what the human brain can take, and I had long since exceeded mine. I had spent my entire life being strong, pushing forward, and grinding to succeed. But during COVID, all of that was stripped away. I was left with mounting worries - how to pay the bills, how to provide for my family - and with too much time on my hands, my brain went into overdrive.

Pauline could see how bad things had gotten, and she was obviously worried about me. My counsellor, Nicola, knew I was in a dark place and kept a close eye on me. As I said and once again need to make very clear: I would never have taken my own life. I could never put my family through that pain, knowing firsthand what it's like to grow up without a father. But the daily struggle of just putting one foot in front of the other was almost unbearable.

Mental health struggles are not a sign of weakness - they are the body and brain's response to overwhelming stress. Still, I felt weak, broken, and ashamed of my past. I didn't have the strength I was used to relying on, and those were dark, dark days. Everything seemed to come together to break me.

Yet I took it one day at a time. I reached out to Master Martin, Alison, my sister, and, of course, Pauline. They were all amazing, offering me the support I needed to get through that period. I wanted to skip this part of my story because it's so hard to revisit, but I now realise how important it is to acknowledge and process those feelings. There's no shame in struggling - it's only important that you recognise it and seek help.

Reaching out to those you love can give you the strength you need to push through your darkest times. I reminded myself that if I had survived everything from my early life, I could survive this too. Each day, I focused on small steps: long walks, regular exercise, daily meditation, and speaking openly about how I felt. Slowly but surely, I started to rebuild. Bit by bit, I pieced together a stronger mindset and began to look at the future with more hope.

Of course, revisiting the trauma of my past during sessions with Nicola and while gathering evidence for Redress was never going to be easy. But I kept reminding myself that acknowledging the pain was the only way to begin healing. The pandemic stripped away so much, but it also gave me the time and space to confront the demons that had been lurking in my mind for decades.

Even on my worst days, I told myself: one step at a time, one day at a time. That's how you get through this.

We had finally gathered all the evidence needed for the Redress process. My solicitor told me I had an abundance of supporting material - more than enough to validate everything I had shared. She explained that my medical records backed up my account entirely, documenting everything from the panic attacks I experienced as a teenager to the times I broke down crying at the GP, overwhelmed by life. All of that, she said, was clearly linked to CPTSD. Although I wasn't diagnosed at the time, it had been present for decades, affecting me in ways I couldn't understand or articulate back then.

The records also documented my FND and severe dissociation, matching exactly with what I had described. For the first time in my life, I felt completely validated. Someone had gone through all the evidence and records - dating back to when I first entered the care system - and told me, "Everything you've said is there."

That validation broke me in a way I can't fully explain. It was powerful. Someone else finally understood, finally knew exactly what I had gone through. To hear that what I had been saying all my life was true, backed by documented evidence, sent shivers down my spine. It was overwhelming to feel seen and heard after decades of keeping it all locked away.

The process leading to this point had been long, hard, and painful, but it was also healing. I felt battered and broken but had gained a deeper understanding of the cost of the abuse I endured and its immense impact on my life. After nearly four years, the panel sitting was finally arranged, and the week leading up to their decision was the most stressful of my life.

This wasn't about the money. It never had been. I've never cared much for money. But if the panel awarded me a lesser amount, my mind would have told me they didn't fully understand the cost of the abuse, the toll it had taken on me, or the life I lost because of it. That thought was terrifying, as I knew it could push me into a deep, dark place.

About a week after the panel met to review all the evidence, my solicitor called me. She told me I had been awarded the maximum amount.

If I'd won £100,000 on a scratch card, I would have been ecstatic, jumping around at my luck. But when I heard this news, I didn't feel excitement or joy - I felt relief. Relief that I had finally been heard and understood.

My solicitor said the panel recognised that I had suffered horrendous abuse, and the impact of it was clearly visible in my medical records. That acknowledgment was everything. It wasn't about the money; it was about people knowing the truth of what I went through, about having it officially recorded for history.

What Mrs Nobody did to me, and to so many others, is now documented. Her legacy is one of pain, suffering, fear, and trauma. That's what she left in this world. But despite her abuse, I've spent my life building something worthwhile. I've helped others, created positive change, and brought joy to people's lives.

Whether it's through martial arts, life coaching, teaching anti - bullying workshops in schools, or performing as superheroes for kids battling cancer or serious illnesses, my achievements stand in stark contrast to what Mrs Nobody left behind. I wish she were alive to see how I've outstripped her shallow, worthless life tenfold.

I am not bound by the past. I'm learning to let it go. Writing this book has been part of that process - taking all the bad memories that have swirled around unchecked in my mind for decades and putting them on paper.

Of course, the daily anxiety and ruminating thoughts haven't gone away. They buzz constantly in my brain, and addressing them requires slow, consistent work. Every day, I try to recognise the thought patterns and processes that hold me back. I've always said there isn't enough money in the world to fix this or make it better. Instead, I turn to nature to ease my mind. Long bike rides and walks along the beach have become my solace, moments where I can find peace and joy.

Yes, I have deep scars on my soul from this life, but I've also learned so much about what it means to be human. The true currency in this universe isn't money or material wealth - it's love, kindness, and compassion. Unfortunately, those qualities are in such short supply these days, and I try to teach my students the importance of them every single day.

Just because we are battered, bruised, and broken doesn't mean we have to stay that way. Healing begins with small, daily steps. Trust me, I know how hard it is - I've walked that path. People often say, "What doesn't kill us makes us stronger." I disagree. It should be, "What doesn't kill us gives us the chance to take small steps toward healing and understanding."

The hardest part is making that start - putting one foot in front of the other. Many of the kids I grew up with in care can't even register or talk about what happened to them. I was the same for so many years. But until you confront the demons in your head, you remain stuck in a loop of denial, desperately trying to forget the pain. For me, that strategy didn't work.

Confronting your inner demons requires a strength you have to dig deep to find. I know I will spend the rest of my life battling the thoughts in my head, but I hope they will be gentler with time. I've lost all fear of death - the thing that terrified me as a teenager. Now, I believe we are eternal beings, here to learn, no matter how hard the lessons may be.

Recently, I gave my evidence to the Scottish Child Abuse Inquiry. They asked if I wanted my testimony to remain anonymous, and I said no. I want them to use my name. I am standing up and letting the people who know me see what I went through and what it took to get here. It's time to let the darkness be seen in the light. For too long, it stayed in the shadows, a secret never to be spoken about.

I'm not spending the rest of my life carrying the burden of my past. I want it recorded - what happened, who was responsible, and the impact it had on me and countless others. This is about taking back my power, facing the things I was scared and ashamed to talk about, and letting it all be known.

I'm just one voice in thousands of stories, but if I've learned anything, it's that people who grew up in care are some of the strongest people I've ever met. Life dealt us a brutal start, and we endured daily trauma that most people will never experience. Yet we're still here, still fighting, and still finding ways to make our lives matter.

I was incredibly nervous on the day of giving my testimony to the Scottish Child Abuse Inquiry. I wasn't sure what to expect. The session was held in a conference room at a local hotel. When I arrived, one of the representatives met me in the lobby, which immediately helped put me somewhat at ease. He acknowledged how difficult it would be for me to go through my story and reassured me that I could take as many breaks as I needed. He also explained that the session would take the entire day and that anything I disclosed about named abusers would be passed on to the police. I told him I was fine with that. By this point, I had been working with my solicitor on the Redress process for three to four years, and all the evidence had already been gathered and submitted.

When I entered the room, there were three people from the Inquiry present. We began, and I won't lie - it was one of the hardest things I've ever had to do. Speaking about my darkest experiences to a room of strangers was deeply painful. The session was recorded, and they asked me questions about my life in care, starting from day one.

Some moments were overwhelming, and I broke down several times, but I kept reminding myself that this was something I needed to do. Over the course of six or seven hours, I told them my story. By the end, I felt drained, mentally shattered, and utterly worn out.

They explained that my testimony would be typed up as an official statement, and any information regarding named abusers would be passed on to the police. I told them I had reported the historical abuse to the police in the past, but my experience had been terrible - I was made to feel stupid and dismissed. I made it clear I wouldn't put myself through that again. The Inquiry representatives assured me that they would handle everything sensitively and would schedule a later session for me to review and edit the final statement to ensure it was accurate and that I was happy with it.

A few months later, I returned to go through the statement. Some names had to be redacted because, for me, this process was about telling *my* story - not outing others who had chosen not to come forward yet for their own personal reasons. I respected their choices and wanted to protect their privacy. Everyone who was at Thurso Children's Home during Mrs Nobody's time knows exactly what went on - we've talked about it extensively in recent years.

At the end of the session, I thanked the Inquiry representatives for their time and acknowledged how difficult it must be for them to listen to these kinds of stories day in and day out. They, in turn, thanked me for coming forward and sharing my evidence.

It was surreal to see my entire life laid out in fifty or so typed pages. During one of the breaks, I sat back and thought, *So much pain and suffering, condensed into a handful of pages.* Yet those pages represented my story - the truth of what happened to me. And I was glad that history had been set straight.

When I left the building, I paused outside the door for a moment. I took a deep breath and said to myself, *Now finish your book, let it all go, and move on with the remainder of your life without the burden of the past weighing so heavily on you.*

I'm not naive - I know the effects of what I went through will stay with me until my last breath. But I also know that I confronted it. I brought it into the light of day, and that alone has lifted some of the burden.

For me, this marks the start of true healing. The past will always be there, but it no longer has to take so much of a toll on my present. This is a new chapter - a step toward reclaiming the peace and strength that the abuse tried to take away from me.

Me aged 53 fighting back against life

CHAPTER 24:

REFLECTIONS AND UNDERSTANDING

In life, we all have things from our pasts that haunt us, and for some, burying it deep down is the way they feel they can cope. For me, I had done this most of my life, but like I said, my brain forced me to deal with the issues that had broken me deep from within. It was a painful journey, and I would not have the strength to do it again, but I had the strength to start this healing journey. As time has gone on, I got to the worst possible point in life - I reached rock bottom - confronting the things in my life I had buried so deep. There were many times I thought this was going to overwhelm me, and trust me, it was really, really close. But at the worst time, when everything felt so dark and I had had enough, things started to change.

I started to see things from a third - person perspective and in a new light. When I talked about it, it was as if I was speaking about someone else. I became removed from it, and I could start talking about the abuse without breaking down crying. I started to understand things in a new way and see them for what they really were. Growing up and going through life, I never let anyone in. I was deeply ashamed to be me and the things I had gone through and seen others go through. I thought they were a stain on me, and all the abuse was never to be talked about. Somehow, that would make it all more bearable.

In life, we go through experiences - good and bad - and I have learned that most of the growth and the learning comes from the painful things we go through. We come to this existence to learn lessons and to grow, and sometimes - and I mean a lot of times - the lessons are painful and break us down, but then we learn to cope and, in my case, get stronger.

Now, I'm not there yet - far from it. I still wake in the mornings, sometimes jump out of bed ready to go to war to confront whatever threat has crawled into my room to get me. And then I realise it was just another night terror, thanks to CPTSD, and I can calm down faster. But when I look back on the whole journey and how hard it has been and what it has cost me, I realise I have only one direction to head in - and that's forward. Every day, I focus on the things that heal me. I have confronted the things I was scared of. I went and spoke to strangers and said, "I feel broken, lost and done," and trust me, that's harder than anything you can do in life - to confront your inner darkness and demons and drag them into the light for all to see.

All my secrets I swore I'd never talk about to another living person - the pain to even get the words out of my mouth. I'm a proud Highland man, and that's not an easy thing to do for anyone. I grew up in Thurso, the most northerly town in Scotland, in the seventies, when mental health was not discussed and you were told to shut up and "man up" - but as we all know, that is the worst advice ever.

Now, if I can talk about beatings, sexual abuse, hitting rock bottom with suicidal thoughts, self - destructive thoughts and actions that destroyed so many of the positive things that came my way - then you too can confront the things that hurt you in life and from your past. I have learned that you can only start to heal when you reach out to ask for help. It's not a weakness, it's a strength, as it shows you recognise there is a problem. And rather than suffering in silence until the problem overwhelms you and you become another statistic, reach out, speak to anyone - I mean anyone - and let them know what's going on in your head.

Now, I had been on this healing journey for over four years, and I know it will be my path for the rest of my life. I don't expect anyone to feel sorry for me. In fact, that would break my heart. I just want people to know this happened, and I created an amazing life despite the start I had. And in fact, that gave me the fuel in life to create an extraordinary life, and I can feel proud of myself. Because along my journey to create positivity and success in my life, I have helped thousands of people along the way create a better life for themselves through exercise and positive thinking.

You see, even when we can't see our own achievements, it doesn't mean others can't. Life is so hard for everyone these days. The pressure is everywhere, without all the other bullshit we go through which breaks us. True strength comes from deep within. You dig down deep and remind yourself - even when you despise yourself - that the people around you care for you deeply. You are the reason they smile every day, and that's the reason you speak out about the stuff that's breaking you. There is no shame. There is no guilt. We all need help at some point in life. It's not a weakness to acknowledge you're struggling - it's a strength. And the more you nurture that, the more others will too, and the stigma of opening up that something's wrong will disappear, and we can make it the norm for people to talk about the things that break them.

When I started writing my book, I was in a very different place than I am now. My redress has been completed now, and the Scottish Government recognised what I had gone through and the terrible impact it has taken on my life and my mental health. They recognised my abuse was horrendous, and I will be getting a written apology from them for it.

Now, no amount of money or apology can make up for what happened to me, nor the destructive impact it has had on my life. But for me, it's another wee ray of sunshine I'm slowly adding back into my life - another piece of the healing journey. And just like the Great Pyramids - one block at a time - until I'm complete again.

Getting my records from the home and understanding how little they understood about me and what I went through - but also looking back and realising there were great humans in the children's home as well. Like Christine Gray, who was my angel, a mum God sent me when mine was gone. Val, who used to give me money for the shops for a sweet, out of her own money amazing. Or Izzy, who would take us walks and buy us chips from her own money. Or Mary, or any of the other staff that came later in the home and didn't beat the shit out of us.

Now, as I have said, they were not all like that. And if they are reading this book, they will know who they are. And guess what - if you did ever hit me, I forgive you. Life's too short, and I choose to move on. And like I said, life's a lesson, and maybe they will learn their lesson after all these years.

Mrs Nobody - well, that's a different case. You robbed me of so much in life, but your actions gave me the fire to prove you wrong. And I created what I did with my life - stuff you could never achieve in a million lifetimes.

I also realise now, as I'm fifty-five, even she had a story. And maybe she went through what she dished out. There always is a reason people do the things they do - both good and bad. But you made choices that had long lasting effects on so many people. I am nothing like her and never will be. I bring as much positivity and joy into the world as I can now.

We all mess up in life - that's what it is to be human. It's an experience, and we are meant to learn from it all. If I have brought fifty-one percent happiness into the world and forty-nine percent negative, I can live with that. Every day, I recognise more and more what this journey has meant, what the purpose of my existence has been, and how I have grown in the last four years more than in all I have achieved in my life.

This book is me setting the record straight, regardless of what people may think or say. I couldn't care less. I'm unburdening myself from it all.

People look and say, "Wow, you have created a great life for you and your family," and I'm like, "If you only knew what it took and cost for me to get here - and the fact I'm even here in the first place." I have had people say to me, "It's all right for you - look at what you have in life." I stay quiet and say in my head, "My friend, let me tell you a story that starts in a children's home in the far north of Scotland, with a lady I will call Mrs Nobody." That's what goes through my head. But now I'm telling that story out loud to whoever reads this book. You will understand what this life has cost me to get here.

As I said, I don't care if no one reads this story. For me, it will be on a shelf in my house so I can see if on a daily basis, for however long I have left on this realm. It has taken me out of the darkness, and into the light. Out of my mind and into physical form from now until I'm gone. My story told, with my head held high.

I know there are thousands who went through the same, or worse, in care homes in the seventies, and to anyone that went through it with me - and I know you can't talk about it - if you are struggling with the thoughts in your head, I'm here for anyone, at any time. Just call or message me. And there is amazing help out there - in my case, it was Future Pathways. I will link some help groups at the end of this book.

You are not alone, and you have nothing - I mean *nothing* - to be ashamed of. This happened *to* us, not *because* of us. Remember those words.

I am going to focus the last part of my life on healing - until there is so much sunshine in my soul that I struggle to see the darkness. Long bike rides, going to the gym, spending time with my family, reading and learning - whatever it takes to calm my brain and soul. Practising and teaching martial arts and self - defence. I am also going to start giving talks on my life and what I went through, and the journey to healing, in the hopes it can inspire others who have had similar struggles in their lives.

Because the more we talk, the more people will come forward to share their trauma or life struggles. We *have* to make it normal to share what breaks us. I used to struggle to even start the conversation about abuse - I would cry for hours and struggle to form the words. But now I can just about get through it, and for me, that's a massive step forward.

Will I ever get to a point where I can talk about this without deep sadness? Probably not. But I will definitely be able to talk about it with a new inner strength and passion to help others who went through the same thing. I have already helped three of the kids in the Thurso and Lybster homes start the redress process and help seek the support and help they need to address - and slay - the demons in their head. I'm passionate about that, as I know exactly what it has, and still does, cost them - every second of every day.

I'm now fifty - five, and when I tell people I'm writing a book, they have no idea it's going to be about child abuse, growing up in care, CPTSD or FND - as all they know is about my martial arts or breakdancing or the positive stuff I have done in life that inspires them.

I didn't want to write that kind of book that whitewashes my life to make it seem like it's a life of achievement. I want people to know what it cost - and still costs - me. I want them to know I have struggled from day one. Everything I have done in life, I got the hard way. I was never given anything. I earned it all through hard work, determination, sacrifice, and focus.

I want them to know all my success was down to me feeling worthless, being disgusted with myself, and the shame I felt about my past - and the hatred I had for being *me*. Even though they remember me smiling and being happy, behind my smile there is a story you could never understand, because words do not let you feel the pain, self - loathing, and hatred I felt for myself.

I became a master of martial arts - but long before that, I became a master of putting on a smile and pretending I was not broken.

Think about the worst moment in your life, when you were not proud of yourself, and you felt you let everyone down, and you fell short, and people were disappointed in you. Now really focus on how you felt - and multiply that by ten. That's how I felt *all the time*. Every second of every day - even when I was laughing with my friends, even when I was dancing in front of hundreds of people clapping, even when I won business awards and all my family and friends were around me celebrating my achievements.

On the outside, I was overjoyed. But on the inside, I was not worthy. I was a fake and did not deserve any of it. That's the cost of the abuse - a lifetime of pain.

But now, I'm starting to reprogramme my mind. I'm trying to be kinder to myself. I'm reminding myself that thinking that way - the loathing and hatred - was beaten into me. It was reinforced with words like "useless," "unworthy," and "stupid."

I'm changing it to *survivor*, *warrior*, *worthy*. And each day, I'm getting stronger and facing up to the things I never wanted to talk about.

I had a choice - to write a whitewashed book hiding all the dark stuff, or the book you are reading, that is from my soul, as I experienced it - all the good, and all the bad. There are plenty of crazy stories I have left out of the book due to size, but they are for another day.

I'm aware my family will read my book. My son will read it and learn things I wanted to keep away from him. But in reading this, Jay, you will learn that the path Dad took to get here was painful and hard - but confronting the things that are hard in life is where the true strength lies. And it's okay to not be okay in life sometimes. But reaching out is the greatest thing you can do.

And for many of my friends I grew up with - they had absolutely no idea what was going on, as I hid it and put on my smile and got on with it. Well, now everyone that reads this will know that this was not an easy journey, and I have grown from it - even though it has been, by far, the hardest, most painful thing I have ever done.

Mental health, for years, was something we never talked about, as for many it was perceived as a weakness. Now, there are groups set up to provide the help and support we all may need at some time in our lives, and I hope if my book does anything, it can reach out to anyone who feels their struggles are getting the better of them.

I promise you - our mind is not our best friend. Now say that one more time out loud... *"My mind is not my best friend."* Sometimes, our brains think in an unhealthy way, and we need to recognise that and train it like we would a new puppy - train the behaviours that nurture positive thoughts, and use thinking strategies to keep us healthy and positive in life.

The sooner we realise it's okay not to be okay, the better. Remember, your greatest strength in life is you. But like me, I know sometimes you just can't see it. We need a little loving help to get back on track - and that's not only good, but it's also bloody amazing.

Your strength is recognising when to ask for support and help. Learn to reach out. I often wonder where I would be if I had not reached out for help from the ones I love. I hate to think - but I did, and now I'm on the path to a better future.

On my Facebook page, I write my life thoughts - whatever is going through my head. These are actually notes for myself about being positive and working hard to create the best version of myself. People read them and say, "What a beautiful thing to write," and in turn, I convert that energy into beautiful thoughts in my head. That makes me feel better about myself and helps calm the negative thoughts.

Whatever things get you to where you need to be - nurture the things that make you stronger. And the weeds? The weeds are the thoughts where you put yourself down. Dig them up and throw them out. Be a gardener in your own mind. Cultivate happiness, and the more you do it, the better you become.

The more time you spend recognising the negative stuff, the better you will be at gaining control over the thoughts running through your head. It's not easy, but if we practise every day, it helps. We don't have to be perfect in life. Just getting up each day and trying your best is enough - and when you've had a hard life, that's a victory in itself.

I look back to when I was in my twenties, and I used to think I could fly. I had so much energy and enthusiasm for self - improvement. I was driven and focused on the pursuit of improvement - but that was all physical. I had no concept of mental health. I just shut it all down.

I wish I could go back, just for a day, to help start that healing process then. But that's hindsight - we all have that. It's part of what it is to be human, or the human experience. We live, we learn, and we grow. And then we look back and beat ourselves up for the mistakes we made in life, with the knowledge we have now. It's a strange thing.

But I have learned over the years - we are all looking for growth and self - improvement, and we compare *now* with *then*. And that's not the way to do it. Because back in your past, you did the best you could do with the information you had then.

So slowly, I'm learning not to beat myself up for things I could have maybe done better. Because no - I did the best I could at the time, with the knowledge I had. Maybe this was part of my journey. The self - enlightening that only comes through the pain of realising the past. So, be kind to yourself. I'm learning to do that to myself now, after all of this life journey.

Healing can only come with time and experience, and as we reflect on our lives, we use the past to shape our futures. So, I have made decisions about my future based on the growth and development I have gained in the last four years, going through this healing journey.

As I have said - it was the hardest, most painful thing I have ever done. Facing my biggest demons in life and talking about things I swore would stay in the dark forever. But you see, sometimes we have to *be* the light, to get rid of the things deep down that break us.

Future Pathways, who have helped me so much, and Nicola, my case worker, who was amazing - without them, I don't know where I would have been. And I made a big decision today. As Nicola is leaving Future Pathways, I was due to meet and get a new counsellor. But I feel, as I near the end of this book - and the self - discovery and understanding I have gained into myself and the abuse I suffered, through the cathartic healing of writing a book which makes you go through every strand of your life with more understanding eyes - it's like the many threads come together to help you not just start the healing journey, but to understand what it all meant.

The impact on your life and mental health.

I realised I have reached a point where I will leave Future Pathways with the knowledge I have gained over the last four years to continue each day towards a happier, healthier way of thinking about trauma and the way my brain has responded in order to protect itself from the things it did not want to face.

I am making a deal with myself: keep healing every day. Be a bit easier on myself.

And now, I have started the journey. I went through all the gathering of evidence for redress with my solicitor. I had my suffering acknowledged and proven by my solicitor and the Scottish Government. The battles for my records, the giving of evidence to the Scottish Child Abuse in Homes Enquiry, Future Pathways, the psychologists, the evidence from my medical records - *all of it* has taken me to the point where I realise it will never go away completely.

But I now recognise the toll it took on me, and I'm moving forward - to let go of the past and finally be at one with it all.

Writing this book has been amazing for my soul, and I hope if you are reading this, you can understand the cost abuse has on a sufferer's life - but above all else, how hard I worked in my life to prove I was worthwhile, and that I was a survivor of the things that should never have happened all those years ago.

Now, I look forward to seeing my finished book as my greatest personal life achievement. I'm still waiting for the treatment for my CPTSD - that's been a year and a half now, so still a while yet. But I'm in a whole lot better place than I was a couple of years ago.

Sometimes in life, we must dig really deep to get ourselves out of a hole - and whatever way you can find the strength to do that, grasp it with both hands. That's where personal growth comes from. Sometimes, it's the most painful thing you will ever do, as you must confront the things that broke you in the first place.

I felt I no longer needed to explain my story to another counsellor. I have been there and done that, and there comes a time when, to heal, you have to have understanding - but also look to closure at the right time. Learning to move forward, or you become stuck in the perpetual retelling of things that hurt you. I have addressed the things in my life I did not want to, and I'm in a much stronger place than I could have ever believed possible. But I'm also smart enough to realise you can never fully heal from something like that. You just learn to understand and cope better than you did before. But you can never let your guard down, as the battle is lifelong.

That was what was inflicted on me, my brother and sister, and the other kids that lived in the Lybster home and early Thurso - who have since come forward to tell me about the horrors that went on - and the kids that went through Mrs Nobody's brand of "care."

I have learned that what I thought was a shameful stain on who I was is actually a shame on who *they* were. I have also learned that it's okay not to be okay, as long as you don't give in - and find the strength and support from whoever makes you feel you can keep going on.

True strength was not all the thousands of hours perfecting my body and skills, but rather, the true strength was confronting my past and learning and growing from it - even though you realise the hurt it caused others through pushing them away and self - isolating and all the other stuff. Now, I enjoy solitude. Even though I now understand it's a response to the past, it is my happy place and always will be. I have grown used to the comfort of solitude and the safety of being alone - and although that's a relic of the past, it will be with me until my last day on this realm.

I think it's the one way I can make sense of and cope with all that's happened - and you know what? I can live with that. It's who I am now, and it's how I cope without being overwhelmed with life.

You see, we are like patchwork quilts made up from all the events, both good and bad, that happened in our lives. And sometimes, the threads that hold all that together, for whatever reason, become frayed and things start to fall apart - and we have to mend the threads that hold our lives together.

None of us are immune to the things in our lives that are most painful, but we all have the ability to reach out and ask for help - or to give help and support to others. Kindness is very important to me, as my life lacked that in my early years. So now, anytime I can do an act of kindness, I do. It's therapeutic to put a smile on someone's face, and the more you do it, the more you yourself will smile.

I'm now dedicating time to help others I know who suffered a hard start like mine, to seek and find the justice and help that I know, in my life, has helped me see this all in a new light. And hopefully, when the time is right, they can start their healing journey too - as I know what they go through daily.

My son Jay has inherited that from both me and Pauline, and I love seeing how kind and caring he has become. Because imagine if we all did that - one act of kindness every day - then maybe the world would be a wee bit better. I sound like I'm turning into a hippie in my old age, but I believe that kindness and love is how we fix a lot of the world's problems now - and we should all lead by example.

When I go back home every year to Thurso, I go by the old children's home on Ormile Road, and there are so many conflicting memories. The terror and fear of Mrs nobody, to the love of Christine Grey and the later staff that were so good to us. Strange how a building you grew up in can invoke so many memories - both the good, the bad, and the terrible. But now, I remember the positive and slowly let the bad memories wither away and die, day by day.

No one will understand how hard the journey has been - and that's okay. It was not their journey or life story, but mine. And again, I'm at ease with that. I came here not for an easy life, but a challenging one - but for sure, a worthwhile one too.

I can see, over the years, the impact my early life had on the way I perceive the world. But my lesson was to learn and accept and gain control over my early start in life. That's where my greatest strength would come from.

As I write this, it's the anniversary of Christine's death. I have a tear rolling down my cheek. I just wish she was here so I could share my journey with her, as she had the best advice and always knew what to say to make me feel better about myself.

The hardest part in life is we all lose loved ones - it's a part of being human. Grief and sadness seem a part of why we are here and what it means to be human. But then I remind myself - so is love, joy, and happiness. And I know Christine would never want me feeling sorry for myself or sad. But sometimes grief rolls down our cheeks and drips off our chins without us being aware. I like to think that's all the love we have for a person just making itself known. And we would never appreciate our loved ones without knowing the pain of losing them. That's the balance of the universe. That's the teaching and understanding of being a soul in human form.

From this day onwards, I hold my head high. I've done the best job I could with the hand I was given. Have I made mistakes and could I have done things differently? Sure - but couldn't we all say that?

On my last day on Earth, and when I look back, I wouldn't change anything. Who I became, and what I am, and the impact I have had on so many - both good and bad - is part of my tapestry. It's the blanket of my life, woven with pain, loss, hardship and suffering - but also great achievement, and overcoming things I thought I couldn't, and bringing joy to many.

So - no regrets. I am me, and I did the best I could. And I can live with that.

So, the unwanted gift brought me to a point of deep understanding of who I am and why I'm here. It helped me achieve an amazing life, despite the fact it should have gone in a very different direction. I've seen the worst in people - but also the very best. And one thing I know - it's been a crazy ride, and I'm just glad I got here, to fifty - five, with an amazing family and a good life with good people in it - the right people.

I have no fear of death now and feel I have completed my life mission. I can take a deep breath and let go. Writing my story is another chapter in my life, and another thing ticked off my bucket list. Over the years, people who knew me said, "You should write a story about your life." And I used to think, *I'll never tell people my inner thoughts*. But now, here they are. The inner thinking of my views on my life - for all to see.

I look forward to the next stage of my life, going forward and leaving the past behind. Trying to have some peace for my soul.

The battle is over, even though I will always remain vigilant. I never gave up fighting, and in the end - I won the war.

If this book has helped you see life or people differently - if it's changed your perception of what strength truly is - I'd be incredibly grateful if you could leave a review on Amazon or Goodreads.

Sharing what you've taken from this story could help others find the courage to speak up about their own.

Never judge someone by the chapter of their story you walked in on. You never know what came before - until you've read the whole book.

ACKNOWLEDGEMENTS

To my partner, **Pauline Rae**, who has helped me through the toughest times of my life and is always there for me, unconditionally.

To my beautiful son, **Jay**, for making me a father and allowing me to be the best version of myself—without even knowing it.

To my instructors, **Master Alison** and **Master Martin**, for their years of guidance, support, and wisdom.

To my boxing coach, **Frank McShane**, for his inspiration and relentless work ethic.

To my **brother and sisters**—I love you always.

To my old-school **breakdance pals** from both Thurso and Wick, for letting me be myself and never asking for explanations.

To all the **instructors** who shared their knowledge and helped shape me into the martial artist I became—thank you.

To **Thurso**, which will always hold a special place in my heart.

To **Master Gavin Chung**, my most loyal friend through the years—thank you from the bottom of my heart.

To all my **black belts** over the years—your support never goes unnoticed.

To my **loyal students**, past and present—thank you for allowing me to teach and grow with you.

To my incredible **superhero team**—you are the best, and I'm so proud of what we've built together.

To **Joan Elder** and **Joan Miller**, for opening your homes to me as a teenager and showing me the love and support I needed so badly at the time. Also to Joan Reid and Dougie Reid.

To **Ally Gray** and **Christine's family**, for all the kindness you've shown me over the years.

A special thank you to **Future Pathways** for their help and support, and for funding this project, as well as to **Mary Turner Thomson** of **The Book Whisperers** (www.thebookwhisperers.com) for her expert advice and guidance in creating this book with me. If you've lived through trauma, I thoroughly recommend writing it down. It's surprising how much healing it can bring - it has helped me more than I ever imagined.

And finally... To **Christine Gray** - you guided my life, always supported me, and were always there for me. You were the mum I never had. I miss you more than words can say.

To find out more about my businesses please see:
www.martialarts-ksw.co.uk

To get in touch you can do so by emailing me at:
don_mackenzie2000@yahoo.com

Printed in Dunstable, United Kingdom